Italy Tr

MW00935387

Explore the Country &

Speak Italian Like a Local!

3 Books in 1

Explore to Win

THIS COLLECTION INCLUDES THE FOLLOWING BOOKS:

Rome Travel Guide

Florence Travel Guide

Venice Travel Guide

BONUS: Italian Phrase Book

Table of Contents

$100+ FREE BONUSES

**Italy Audio
Pronunciations**

**Italy Travel
Hacking Guide**

**Italy Travel Hacks
Audiobook**

**Italy Visual
Travel Guide**

**Italy Travel
Itineraries**

**Italy Budget
Travel Guide**

Scan QR code to claim
your bonuses

—— OR ——

visit bit.ly/3QdAjfJ

Book 1

Rome Travel Guide

Explore to Win

Introduction

Are you ready to plunge headfirst into a grand theater of human history, an ageless city where tales are told through cobblestones, the very air vibrates with an ancient rhythm, and the echoes of a thousand narratives resonate in the whispering wind? Well, tighten your shoelaces and adjust your sunhat, for we're about to embark on an extraordinary journey through the streets of Rome, the Eternal City that has captured hearts and imaginations for millennia.

Rome is not just a city; it is a time machine, a living, breathing museum that harbors the soul of Western civilization within its ancient walls. From the bustling cafes along the cobbled streets, filled with laughter, lively conversation, and the aroma of rich espresso, to the grand piazzas echoing with the footsteps of countless generations, Rome is more than a place. It is an experience, a sensory overload of sights, sounds, tastes, and stories that have shaped history.

As you navigate the cobbled labyrinth of Rome's picturesque streets, do you feel a twinge of anxiety or a fluttering pang of uncertainty in your heart? The language barrier seems like a mountain, the cultural nuances akin to a cryptic puzzle, and the vast, complex cityscape a maze with no beginning or end. You're not alone. We've been there too, and we understand. Understanding Rome is not merely a matter of being able to ask for directions or order a meal. It's about deciphering the very soul of the city, unraveling its mysteries, and becoming a part of its rhythmic narrative.

We, the team at Explore To Win, are here to be your guides, confidantes, and cheerleaders on this journey. We're not just language enthusiasts or experienced travelers, we're unabashed Italophiles who've spent years living, breathing, and loving everything Rome has to offer. We've tasted every Roman dish from carbonara to carciofi alla Romana, meandered through every alleyway, engaged in countless conversations with locals, and even debated fiercely about the best gelato flavors. Our passion for Rome has only intensified with each journey, and now, we're here to share this passion, our knowledge, and our experiences with you.

So, what can you expect from this guide? This is not just a book; it's a treasure chest brimming with insider knowledge, engaging narratives, and essential Italian phrases that are your golden ticket to unlocking the Rome that tourists seldom get to see. We delve deeper than the popular landmarks, venturing into the heart of Rome's neighborhoods, markets, festivals, and secret hideaways. Each chapter is a new adventure, revealing not just the sights and sounds of Rome, but the soul of this captivating city.

Alongside, we're handing you the keys to an interactive treasure - Google Maps marked with every location our chapters cover. From the mighty Colosseum to a hidden, snug café, you can virtually stroll through it all, mapping your journey in advance. And here's the golden tip: don't forget to download the map on your device for offline use. That's right! You don't need an internet connection to access your downloaded maps. This way, you can keep your bearings, even in the deepest, most charming corners of Rome, where Wi-Fi might be as elusive as an emperor's ghost.

So, are you ready to explore Rome like never before? Are you ready to step off the beaten path, immerse yourself in Rome's rich culture and history, and experience the city on a level few tourists do? If your heart says a resounding 'yes', then let's turn the page. A grand

Roman adventure awaits you, and we can't wait to be a part of it. Together, we will not just visit Rome, we will live Rome. Let's embark on this journey and explore to win. Ready, set, andiamo!

Chapter 1: Ciao, Roma! An Italian Language Survival Guide

"You may have the universe if I may have Italy."

- Giuseppe Verdi

Italians love to talk. If words were gelato, Italy would be the biggest gelateria in the world! Now, we know what you're thinking - "How do I even start ordering my stracciatella in the midst of all this chatter?" Fear not, friend! We are about to arm you with an essential toolkit of Italian phrases and basic rules that will have you chatting away faster than an Italian sports car on the Autostrada.

In this chapter, we're going to give you the keys to unlock the magic of the Italian language. We'll introduce you to essential Italian phrases and rules that are going to turn you from a mute spectator into a vivacious participant in this magnificent Italian opera. We'll make sure that you won't just be nodding along, you'll be actively involved, ordering your caffe macchiato with an authentic Italian accent that even the barista will appreciate!

So, sit back, relax, and fasten your seatbelts as we embark on this exhilarating journey to master the Italian language. Ready to channel your inner Italian? Perfecto! Let's get this language party started!

Greetings and Polite Expressions

Starting a conversation right is the secret sauce to smooth communication. Italians appreciate courtesy, and a polite phrase here and there goes a long way in warming hearts.

- Good day/Hello: "Buongiorno" (bwohn-johr-noh) - Your all-purpose day greeting until around 4 pm. After that, switch to "Buonasera" (bwoh-nah-seh-rah), which means good evening.

- Goodbye: "Arrivederci" (ah-ree-vuh-dehr-chee) - For saying goodbye to new friends and the waiter who keeps refilling your wine glass.

- Please: "Per favore" (pehr fah-voh-reh) - Remember this, and you might find an extra scoop of gelato in your cone.

- Thank you: "Grazie" (graht-see-eh) - For when someone passes you the last slice of pizza.

Ordering Food and Drinks

One cannot simply survive on words alone - you need your pasta and vino too! Here are phrases to help you tackle the delightful challenge of Italian cuisine.

- I would like: "Vorrei" (vohr-ray) - The magic word that precedes your food or drink order.

- A table for two, please: "Un tavolo per due, per favore" (oon tah-voh-loh pehr doo-eh, pehr fah-voh-reh) - The key to securing that romantic dinner.

- The bill, please: "Il conto, per favore" (eel kohn-toh, pehr fah-voh-reh) - But remember, good things (like tiramisu) often come last.

Navigating Around

If you're worried about getting lost, remember that all roads lead to Rome! Still, knowing how to ask for directions can come in handy.

- Where is...?: "Dove si trova...?" (doh-veh see troh-vah) - Because knowing where the nearest gelateria is, is a matter of utmost importance!

- Left: "Sinistra" (seen-eest-rah), Right: "Destra" (deh-strah) - Crucial for when you're navigating the winding streets of Trastevere.

In Case of Emergency

Italy is generally safe, but it's essential to be prepared. Keep these phrases handy.

- Help!: "Aiuto!" (ah-yoo-toh) - Just in case you find yourself in a Roman Holiday-style Vespa chase!

- I need a doctor: "Ho bisogno di un dottore" (oh bee-zohn-yoh dee oon doht-toh-reh) - For non-pizza related emergencies!

Alright, get ready for a crash course in Italian 101! Don't worry, we promise this won't be as nerve-racking as sitting in a Roman cafe and not knowing your caffe americano from your cappuccino. We're going to cover the basics of Italian grammar - things like pronouns, verbs, and how to ask questions.

Italian Pronouns

These little words are the stand-ins for nouns. They're your "I," "you," "he," "she," "we," "it," and "they" of the Italian language. Italian pronouns are also marked for politeness, and the formal "you" uses the same form as "she". Here's a detailed list of Italian subject pronouns to get you started:

- I: Io (ee-oh)
- You (singular, informal): Tu (too)
- He: Lui (loo-ee)
- She: Lei (lay)
- You (singular, formal): Lei (lay)
- We: Noi (noy)
- You (plural, informal): Voi (voy)
- You (plural, formal): Loro (loh-roh)
- They (masculine and feminine): Loro (loh-roh)

In the formal context, "Lei" is used regardless of the gender of the person you're addressing. This might seem odd, but it's one of the fascinating aspects of Italian language and culture. When using the formal "Lei," remember to also conjugate the verb in the third-person singular, as if you were saying "she."

Moreover, when referring to "they," Italians use "Loro," regardless of whether the group is all male, all female, or mixed. And when you're addressing a group formally, you would use "Loro," but this is becoming less common, especially in the spoken language.

Italian Verbs

The meat and potatoes of any language, verbs are action words. In Italian, regular verbs fall into three categories, depending on their endings: -are, -ere, and -ire. For example:

- Parlare (to speak)
- Leggere (to read)
- Aprire (to open)

The tricky bit is that these verbs change depending on who is doing the action. For instance, "I speak" is "Io parlo", while "You speak" is "Tu parli". Notice the ending change? We'll delve deeper into verb conjugation later, but for now, just remember that verbs like to dress differently depending on who they're going out with!

Asking Questions

Asking questions is crucial when you're navigating a new city, whether you're looking for the Colosseum or the best gelato in town. Here are a few key question words:

- What?: Che cosa? (keh koh-zah)
- Where?: Dove? (doh-veh)
- When?: Quando? (kwahn-doh)
- Why?: Perché? (pehr-keh)
- Who?: Chi? (kee)

Stick one of these at the beginning of a sentence and you've got yourself a question. For instance, "Dove il Colosseo?" becomes "Where is the Colosseum?"

Insider Tips

- Order Like a Roman: Ordering a latte will get you a glass of milk! For a milky coffee, ask for a "caffè latte."

- Afternoon Coffee: Italians usually have their coffee strong, short, and several times a day. But after lunch or dinner, "un caffè" (a coffee) means an espresso.

- Complimenting the Chef: If you've just had a great meal, use the phrase "Complimenti al cuoco!" (compliments to the chef). It's a great way to show appreciation for good food!

- Understanding Meal Structure: The Italian meal structure typically includes antipasti (appetizers), primi (first course, often pasta), secondi (second course, usually meat or fish), and dolci (desserts). It helps to know this when looking at a menu.

- Tipping in Rome: Tipping isn't as common in Italy as in other countries. Service is usually included in the bill, but if you've received exceptional service, feel free to leave a few extra euros.

- Paying the Bill: When you're ready to pay, say "Il conto, per favore" (The bill, please). If you're sharing the bill with friends, you can say "Possiamo dividere il conto?" (Can we split the bill?)

- Street Talk: Romans have a distinctive way of speaking, even compared to other Italians. For an authentic Roman experience, try picking up local Romanesco phrases like "Daje" (Come on), "Aò" (Hey), or "Ammazza!" (Wow!).

- Aperitivo Time: "Aperitivo" (similar to happy hour) is a pre-dinner ritual in Rome, usually between 7 and 9 pm. During this time, you can enjoy cocktails with small appetizers. Try an "Aperol Spritz" or a "Negroni" and enjoy la dolce vita!

- Familiarize Yourself with Directions: In Rome, you'll find "municipio" signs, indicating the district you're in. Knowing the "municipio" can help you understand better where you are. There are currently 15 municipi in Rome.

Key Takeaways

- Essential Italian Phrases:

  - Greetings and Polite Expressions: Remember your "Buongiorno," "Arrivederci," "Per favorer," and "Grazie."
  - Ordering Food and Drinks: "Vorrei" is your new best friend at Italian cafes, along with "Un tavolo per due, per favore" and "Il conto, per favore."
  - Navigating Around: "Dove si trova...?" will be your compass in Rome, guiding you left (sinistra) and right (destra).
  - In Case of Emergency: "Aiuto!" and "Ho bisogno di un dottore" could be life savers.

- Italian Pronouns:

  - The stand-ins for nouns: "Io," "Tu," "Lui," "Lei," "Noi," "Voi," and "Loro."

- Italian Verbs:

  - Regular verbs end in -are, -ere, and -ire, and they change according to the subject of the sentence.

- Asking Questions:

- o Key question words: "Che cosa?," "Dove?," "Quando?," "Perché?," and "Chi?".

With these essentials in your pocket, you're well-equipped to venture into the heart of Rome. Keep practicing and remember that every mistake is just another step toward fluency. Remember, we have included the full list of these verbs with their pronunciations and conjugations in our handy digital resource. Andiamo, amico! We have an exciting journey ahead of us.

Exercises

1. Fill in the blank: Buon _____ (Good morning)

2. Multiple Choice: What is the Italian word for 'Thank you'?
   A) Merci B) Gracias C) Grazie D) Danke

3. True or False: 'Prego' in Italian means 'Please'.

4. Fill in the blank with the correct Italian pronoun: _____ sono Marco. (_____ am Marco)

5. Multiple Choice: How do you say 'Where is the bathroom?' in Italian?
   A) Dov'è la cucina? B) Dov'è il bagno? C) Dov'è la biblioteca? D) Dov'è l'aeroporto?

6. True or False: 'Si' means 'Yes' in Italian.

7. Fill in the blank: Buona _____ (Good night)

8. Multiple Choice: How do you say 'Goodbye' in Italian?
   A) Hola B) Au Revoir C) Ciao D) Sayonara

9. True or False: 'Arrivederci' is a casual way to say goodbye.

10. Fill in the blank: _____ parla inglese? (Do you speak English?)

11. Multiple Choice: What does 'Non capisco' mean in English?
    A) I don't understand B) I don't know C) I don't want D) I don't like

12. True or False: 'Scusa' can be used to say, 'Excuse me'.

13. Fill in the blank: Parlo un po' di _____ (I speak a little
    _____)

14. Multiple Choice: Which phrase is used for 'I need help'?
    A) Ho bisogno di un caffè B) Ho bisogno di aiuto C) Ho
    bisogno di una pizza D) Ho bisogno di un gatto

15. True or False: 'Quanto costa?' means 'How much does it
    cost?'

Answer Key

1. Giorno
2. C) Grazie
3. False, 'Prego' means 'You're welcome'.
4. Io
5. B) Dov'è il bagno?
6. True
7. Notte
8. C) Ciao
9. False, 'Arrivederci' is a formal way to say goodbye.
10.   Lei
11. A) I don't understand
12. True
13. Italiano
14. B) Ho bisogno di aiuto
15. True

Chapter 2: Delving into Rome: Layers of History, Culture, and Vibrancy

"Rome was a poem pressed into service as a city."

– Anatole Broyard

Welcome, dear adventurer, to your second stop on this Italian journey - a deep dive into the heart of Rome's riveting history, tantalizing culture, and buzzing vibrancy.

Rome, the Eternal City, didn't earn its nickname just because it sounds nice. It's the tangible layers of history that make it so 'eternal.' It's like an onion but far less tear-inducing and much more fascinating. Each layer you peel back reveals a different era of history, a new set of stories, and a unique part of Rome's character. The ruins of ancient Rome coexist with medieval piazzas, Renaissance fountains, and modern-day gelaterias. It's a heady mix of time periods that only adds to Rome's distinct flavor.

Romulus, Remus, and the Wolf: The Mythical Beginnings

Rome, 753 BC. As the story goes, Romulus and Remus, the twin sons of Mars, the god of war, were left to die but were saved by a she-wolf. Eventually, Romulus founded the city and named it after himself.

Ancient Rome: Togas and Gladiator Sandals

Fast forward a few hundred years, and we're in the thick of Ancient Rome. Think Julius Caesar, gladiatorial battles, and some serious architectural prowess. The Colosseum, Roman Forum, and the Pantheon all hail from this era.

Medieval Rome: From Empire to Papal State

As the Western Roman Empire fell, Rome lost its political power, but gained religious prominence. It became the center of the Catholic Church, and beautiful basilicas, like St. Peter's, started to pop up.

Renaissance and Baroque Rome: When Art Blossomed

Rome in the Renaissance and Baroque period was a hive of artistic activity. Bernini, Michelangelo, and Caravaggio left their mark on the city with sculptures, paintings, and architectural wonders.

Introduction to contemporary Roman life and customs

It's time to return to the 21st century and uncover what it really means to be a Roman today.

La Dolce Vita

"La Dolce Vita," or "the sweet life," isn't just a Fellini film; it's a way of life for Romans.

Food – The Universal Language

Whether it's a Nonna sharing her secret pasta recipe or friends breaking bread together at a local trattoria, food is a way for Romans to connect with each other and their heritage.

Passeggiata – A Stroll with Style

After dinner, you'll often see Romans indulging in a "passeggiata," a leisurely stroll around the neighborhood.

The Art of Sprezzatura

The Italian concept of 'Sprezzatura' is about making everything look effortless, from your style to your demeanor. To blend in, try to adopt this nonchalant elegance.

Il Calcio Storico

This historic football game is a wild, energetic mash-up of soccer, rugby, and wrestling. While not in Rome, it's a short trip to Florence and an amazing experience if you're in Italy during June.

La Passeggiata in Garbatella

While La Passeggiata is a well-known Italian tradition, doing it in the unique neighborhood of Garbatella gives you a less touristy and more authentic experience.

Key Takeaways

- **Rome wasn't built in a day, nor was its history:** In our brief historical tour, we uncovered that Rome had been the center stage of civilization for centuries.

- **A walk through Rome is a walk through time:** Visiting Rome can feel like time-traveling. "This constant dance between the past and present gives Rome its unique charm and energy.

- **The contemporary Roman life is as enticing as its history:** Embrace the Roman 'dolce vita' (sweet life) lifestyle – relish a long, leisurely dinner, sip on a coffee in a picturesque piazza, and let Rome work its magic on you.

Chapter 3: Rome's Ancient Landmarks

"Rome – the city of visible history, where the past of a whole hemisphere seems moving in funeral procession with strange ancestral images and trophies gathered from afar."

- George Eliot

Welcome to Chapter 3, "Echoes of the Empire: Rome's Ancient Landmarks," the chapter where we swap our espresso for a helmet and our scooter for a chariot. Here, we'll be transporting you back a couple of millennia, to a time when togas were in vogue, chariot racing was the sport of choice, and 'tweet' meant the sound a bird makes. Now buckle up, time travelers, let's unleash our inner Indiana Jones and get ready to explore the eternal city's ancient treasures!

The Colosseum

Imagine this: You're sitting on the edge of your marble seat, heart pounding, as you watch gladiators with muscles on their muscles duke it out below. Suddenly, a lion is let loose onto the sands, and the crowd goes wild, and at that moment, you can't help but think, "Did I really leave my cozy home for this?!"

Fast forward to the present day, and fortunately for us, the lion and gladiator fights have been replaced with peaceful tours, audio guides, and an abundance of selfie opportunities. The Colosseum stands tall and proud, a monument to Roman engineering genius, and a tantalizing window into the lives of our ancient ancestors.

Practical Info:

- Location: Piazza del Colosseo, 1, 00184 Roma RM, Italy.
- Getting There: A short stroll from the Colosseo metro station. Beware of gladiators seeking selfies!
- Ticket Prices: €24 - equivalent to four cappuccinos at a trendy café, or one tourist-trap gelato! Purchase online to dodge the lines.
- Operating Hours: Open from 8:30 AM to one hour before sunset, unless Caesar's ghost hosts a party.
- Tours: Fancy a journey back in time? Opt for a guided tour. Togas are optional.
- Baggage Check: Leave your life-size gladiator armor at home, bulky items are a no-no.
- Restrooms and Facilities: Available at the entrance and within the site. Thankfully, they've been updated since Roman times!
- Recommended Time to Spend: Allocate at least two hours. If visiting the Roman Forum and Palatine Hill, make it a half day.

The Roman Forum

Rome's forum was the heart of its public life – imagine it as a blend of a bustling market, a grand stage for public speeches, a place for trials, and, of course, a setting for those classic "Et tu, Brute?" moments.

As you walk amongst the ruins, you'll stumble upon the remnants of grand temples, basilicas, and arches. Take the Temple of Saturn, for instance. Once Rome's national bank, it would be the equivalent of finding a 2,500-year-old Wall Street.

Now, as you tread through the Via Sacra (Sacred Road), close your eyes and imagine the triumphal processions that once echoed through these streets, the cheers of the crowds, the clinking armor of the Roman legions, the lavish displays of spoils from distant lands.

Just remember one thing: while walking through these ancient streets, if you come across a suspicious-looking knife, don't pick it up. It might be the one Brutus used on a certain March day. Best to leave the souvenirs to the gift shop!

Practical Info:

- o Location: Via della Salara Vecchia, 5/6, 00186 Roma RM, Italy.
- o Getting There: Located in the city center, a short walk from the Colosseo metro station.
- o Ticket Prices: Regular ticket costs €24, and includes entry to the Colosseum and Palatine Hill.
- o Operating Hours: Opens at 8:30 am. Closing time varies depending on the season.
- o Recommended Time to Spend: Allocate at least 2-3 hours.

The Pantheon

This architectural marvel, which has stood the test of time and countless Roman parties, features a circular portico with three ranks of massive granite Corinthian columns.

The Pantheon was initially built as a temple for all gods (hence the name 'Pantheon', from the Greek words 'pan' and 'theion', meaning 'all gods'). But when the Roman Empire swapped its many gods for just one and turned Christian, the Pantheon was converted into a church. And it has been in use ever since!

So, make sure you add the Pantheon to your Roman to-do list. Not just because it's one of the best-preserved Roman buildings but also because it's a master class in Roman ingenuity and style.

Practical Info:

- Location: Piazza della Rotonda, 00186 Roma RM, Italy.
- Getting There: Centrally located in Rome's historic center. Numerous bus lines service the area.
- Ticket Prices: Entry is free, but donations are welcome.
- Operating Hours: Monday to Saturday, 8:30 AM to 7:30 PM. Sunday, 9:00 AM to 6:00 PM. Public holidays, 9:00 AM to 1:00 PM.
- Time to Spend: Most visitors spend around 40 minutes to 1 hour.

Palatine Hill and Circus Maximus

The Palatine Hill is where history oozes from every corner. A tranquil haven away from the city's hustle, offering splendid views of the Roman Forum and Circus Maximus. As you wander its peaceful, tree-lined pathways, remember: you're strolling the same ground where emperors lived, where Rome was born, and, according to legend, where a she-wolf raised two baby boys who would change the world. No biggie, just your average day out in Rome!

Speaking of an average day in Rome, how about a visit to the Circus Maximus? For centuries, Romans would flock here, up to 150,000 at a time, to watch exciting, and often deadly, chariot races. It was a place of adrenaline-pumping thrills, deafening cheers, and some serious horse-powered action.

Getting to Palatine Hill and Circus Maximus

By Metro: Take the Metro Line B and get off at the Circo Massimo stop. From there, it's a short walk to the Circus Maximus and the Palatine Hill.

By Bus: Rome's bus network is extensive, and several routes will get you close to these landmarks. Check with local resources for the most current routes and schedules.

Ticket Prices

Palatine Hill: A combined ticket with access to the Colosseum, Roman Forum, and Palatine Hill costs around 16 euros.

Circus Maximus: It's free! You can stroll the grounds at your leisure, no ticket needed.

Operating Hours

Palatine Hill: Opens daily at 8:30 am, with closing times varying by season. It's best to check ahead for the most accurate times.

Circus Maximus: Being a public park, it's always open. Enjoy a sunrise or sunset here for a truly magical experience.

Tours

Several tour operators offer guided tours of Palatine Hill, often combined with the Colosseum and Roman Forum. This can be a great way to learn more about the history and significance of these sites.

Skip the Line: To avoid long lines, especially during peak tourist season, consider buying a 'skip-the-line' ticket or booking a tour with this feature.

Baggage Check: Large bags and suitcases aren't permitted at Palatine Hill, and there's no baggage check. Pack light!

Restrooms and Facilities: There are restroom facilities available at Palatine Hill. The Circus Maximus, being a public park, does not have restrooms, but there are public facilities nearby.

Time to Spend

Palatine Hill: You'll want at least a couple of hours to really explore and soak in the history here.

Circus Maximus: As a public park, you can spend as little or as long as you like here. Perfect for a leisurely picnic lunch!

Castel Sant'Angelo

Now, imagine this. You're at the Castel Sant'Angelo, and boy, it's an intimidating sight. It looks like it could have played the villain in a Disney movie, the kind that has its own haunting melody every time it appears on screen. You half-expect to see a flurry of bats burst out of the top, but instead, you're greeted with a panoramic view of Rome that makes you question every life decision that hasn't led you here sooner.

As you climb higher, you wonder how it went from a family mausoleum to a fortress to a prison to a papal apartment and now a museum. Talk about an identity crisis, am I right? The walls, if they could talk, would probably need a century to unravel their tales.

Reaching the terrace, you take a break at the small café. Sipping your espresso, you take in the stunning views of the city and, for a moment, you feel like a sentinel watching over Rome - until a pigeon comes along, reminding you who the real masters of this city are.

Practical Info:

- Location: Lungotevere Castello, 50, 00193 Roma RM, Italy.
- Getting There: Short walk from Vatican City, or take Metro Line A to Lepanto or Ottaviano station.
- Ticket Prices: Admission to the castle is around €14. Optional guided tours and audio guides available.
- Operating Hours: Tuesday to Sunday, 9:00 AM to 7:30 PM.
- Time to Spend: Around 2-3 hours.

Lesser-Known Treasures

Centrale Montemartini

If you're tired of stuffy old museums, head to Centrale Montemartini. Housed in Rome's first public electrical power plant, it's where Greek and Roman statues meet industrial machinery.

This museum is often overlooked by tourists, which means you get to enjoy the art in peace. So if you're looking to escape the crowds and still immerse in history, this place is your secret hideaway.

Practical Info:

- Location: Via Ostiense, 106, 00154 Roma RM, Italy.
- Getting There: A 10-minute walk from Garbatella station (Metro Line B).
- Cost: Full admission at €11.
- Operating Hours: Tuesday to Sunday, 9:00 AM to 7:00 PM.
- Time to Spend: From an hour to half a day, depending on interest.

The Aventine Keyhole: Rome's Best-Kept Secret

Imagine peeking through a keyhole, and instead of someone's messy living room, you see a perfectly framed view of St. Peter's Basilica. That's the Aventine Keyhole for you, a 'secret' viewing spot at the Knights of Malta headquarters. It's like a small door to a big world.

Practical Info:

Location: Piazza dei Cavalieri di Malta, Rome, Italy.

Getting There: Bus 160 from Termini Station to the Piazza dei Cavalieri di Malta stop.

Cost: Absolutely free!

Operating Hours: Always open, daylight viewing recommended.

Time to Spend: The wait may be longer than the viewing, but it's worth it!

The Pyramid of Cestius

If you've had your fill of Roman ruins and Renaissance art, why not explore Rome's very own pyramid? Yes, you read that right. The Pyramid of Cestius, a little slice of Egypt in Italy, is a funerary monument for a Roman bigwig with a penchant for all things Egyptian.

Practical Info:

- o Location: Piazza di Porta San Paolo, 00153 Roma RM, Italy.
- o Getting There: It's a 2-minute walk from Piramide metro station.

- Ticket Prices: Free to view from outside. For interior access, guided tours are available from €5.50.
- Operating Hours: Interior tours only on certain days. Check in advance.
- Recommended Time to Spend: Around 30 minutes.

Quartiere Coppedè: The Wonderland of Architecture

This small, whimsical neighborhood is a wild mashup of architectural styles from Art Nouveau to Ancient Greek, all with a dash of pure eccentricity. It's the perfect place for an 'Alice in Architectural Wonderland' experience.

Practical Info:

- Location: Piazza Mincio, 2, 00198 Roma RM, Italy.
- Getting There: Take the metro to Policlinico and walk for about 15 minutes.
- Ticket Prices: Free to wander around.
- Operating Hours: Open 24/7.
- Recommended Time to Spend: A few hours to half a day to fully immerse in the unique atmosphere.

Santa Maria della Concezione Crypts

Got a bone to pick with the typical tourist sites? Visit the Santa Maria della Concezione Crypts. It's like Rome's version of the Catacombs, only smaller, weirder, and with chandeliers made out of human bones.

Practical Info:

- Location: Via Vittorio Veneto, 27, 00187 Roma RM, Italy.
- Getting There: A 10-minute walk from Barberini metro station.

- Ticket Prices: €8.50 for adults, €5 for children aged 6-18, free for children under 6.
- Operating Hours: 9 am-6:30 pm, closed on Thursdays.
- Recommended Time to Spend: About an hour.

Key Takeaways

- **Colosseum:** Rome's mighty amphitheater, famous for its gladiator fights and its cheeky resident cats.
  - ➢ Not a bad place to meet a lion, especially if you're armed with a selfie stick instead of a sword.

- **The Roman Forum:** A field of ruins that was once the heart of the Roman Empire.
  - ➢ It's like an ancient version of Times Square, only with fewer LED screens and more marble columns.

- **The Pantheon:** A 2000-year-old temple that became a church, and today stands as the best-preserved ancient Roman building.
  - ➢ If you find yourself in a sudden rainstorm, its open-air oculus might not be the best place for shelter.

- **Palatine Hill and Circus Maximus:** The birthplace of Rome and the spot for ancient chariot races.
  - ➢ Makes for an ideal venue for reliving the film "Ben Hur" — but we'd advise against it!

- **Castel Sant'Angelo:** Once a mausoleum, then a fortress, and now a museum, this multifaceted landmark is a treasure trove of history.

> Don't forget to practice your royal wave from the rooftop terrace - it's a gesture that befits the panoramic view.

- **Getting there & Practicalities:** Knowing how to navigate to these landmarks, their operating hours, ticket prices, facilities, and suggested time to spend at each location.
  > You now know why wearing comfortable shoes in Rome is as crucial as carrying a map!

- **Italian Phrases:** Key Italian phrases and their historical context that could be helpful while exploring these ancient sites.
  > Now you can ask for directions to the closest gelateria or where Julius Caesar met his untimely end - in Italian!

Remember the words of the famous poet, Rainer Maria Rilke: "The only journey is the one within." So why wait? Get ready, set, and continue your Roman adventure!

Chapter 4: Vatican City: A Beacon of Faith and Art

"Art and religion are, then, two roads by which men escape from circumstance to ecstasy."

- James Baldwin

Now, you might be wondering why we're venturing into Vatican City on our Roman odyssey. And that's a fair question. But consider this - Vatican City is nestled right within Rome's city limits. A stone's throw away from the bustling streets of Rome, and you step into another world, another realm - one of solemn faith, awe-inspiring art, and deep-rooted history.

So, let's dust off our art appreciation glasses and adjust our halo, for we're about to walk through the spiritual and artistic epicenter of the Catholic world. Welcome to Vatican City!

St. Peter's Basilica

When you enter, be prepared for an involuntary gasp, or possibly a "Mamma Mia!" in true Italian fashion. This is no ordinary church, folks! Your humble hometown parish, this is not. With its vast nave, glittering mosaics, and a dome designed by Michelangelo himself (Yes, THE Michelangelo), the Basilica is grandeur embodied.

And you see that bronze canopy over the altar, looking all fancy and towering? That's Bernini's Baldachin. It's said that so much bronze was used to build it that it left the Pantheon roofless!

Oh, and while you're here, don't forget to climb the dome for an unrivaled view of Rome.

Practical Info:

- Location: Vatican City. Nearest Metro station is Ottaviano-S. Pietro on Line A, then a 10-minute walk.
- Operating Hours: Basilica: 7 am - 6:30 pm daily. Dome: 8 am - 5 pm.
- Ticket Prices: Basilica entry is free! Dome visit costs €8 (elevator) or €6 (stairs).
- Facilities: Baggage check available (large bags not allowed inside). Restrooms and facilities for disabled visitors are present.
- Recommended Time to Spend: Approx. 2 hours for Basilica and an additional hour for the Dome.

Tips:

- Remember to dress respectfully - no bare shoulders, knees, or midriffs.

- The best time to visit is early morning or late afternoon to avoid the crowds.
- Consider a guided tour to get in-depth insights about the history and art of the Basilica.
- Don't miss the changing of the Swiss Guards at the front of St. Peter's Square. It happens every day at 8 am and 2 pm and is quite a sight!

The Vatican Museums

Yes, museums with an 's'. This place is not just a single building, oh no, it's a complex of 54 galleries, each stuffed to the gills with masterpieces. So, think of it as an all-you-can-eat buffet of world-class art.

First, you'll venture into the Pio Clementino Museum. Here, you can rub shoulders (but not literally, please) with some of the most famous classical sculptures, including the Laocoön Group, Apollo Belvedere, and the rather underdressed statue of Hermes.

From there, you'll progress through a suite of rooms. The Gallery of Maps, which is really a long corridor, is covered floor to ceiling with detailed topographical maps of Italy. It's like Google Earth, but from the 16th century.

Next, you'll step into the Raphael Rooms, these four rooms were frescoed by Raphael and his pupils, making them some of the most jaw-droppingly beautiful rooms in the entire Vatican.

Practical Info:

- o Location: Vatican City. Near Ottaviano Metro stop on Line A. Buses 49, 32, 81, and 982 also stop nearby.
- o Ticket Prices: Standard entry is €17, reduced entry for children 6-18 and students up to age 25 with valid ID is €8. Free for children under 6 and disabled visitors with their carers.
- o Operating Hours: Monday-Saturday, 9 am - 6 pm (ticket office closes at 4 pm). Closed on Sundays, except for the last Sunday of each month with free entry from 9 am - 2 pm.
- o Tours: A variety of tours available for an additional fee.
- o Facilities: Restrooms and facilities for disabled visitors are available. Large bags, backpacks, and umbrellas must be checked in.
- o Recommended Time to Spend: At least 3-4 hours for a brief tour, a day or two for art enthusiasts.

The Sistine Chapel

Now, you might think to yourself, "Surely, I've seen images of the Sistine Chapel's ceiling in my history books or on Google, it can't be that breathtaking." Oh, you sweet, innocent soul! The moment you crane your neck upwards, your eyes feasting on the vibrant frescoes, you'll understand what all the fuss is about.

With every square inch of the ceiling adorned with dramatic scenes, the Sistine Chapel is like the best pop-up book you ever laid your hands on. And no, there's no pop-up version of it in the gift shop. Trust me, I checked.

As you gaze at the iconic scene of The Creation of Adam, you'll find yourself in a deep existential thought, "Did God and Adam have a high-five moment there?" Just remember to keep these musings to yourself, though. The guards don't take too kindly to loud whispers or giggles echoing around the hallowed hall.

Practical Info:

- o Location: Viale Vaticano, Rome. Short walk from "Ottaviano - Musei Vaticani" Metro stop.
- o Ticket Prices: €17 for standard entry, €21 to skip the lines. Free on the last Sunday of each month (9 am - 2 pm).
- o Operating Hours: Monday-Saturday, 9 am - 6 pm (final entry 4 pm).
- o Tours: Various guided tours available, usually covering the Vatican Museums, St. Peter's Basilica, and the Sistine Chapel.
- o Facilities: Restrooms, cafes, and cloakrooms for larger items are available. Remember the dress code: no bare shoulders, shorts, miniskirts, or hats.

o Recommended Time to Spend: At least half a day to fully appreciate the majesty and soak in all the "holy" details.

Hidden Gems of The Vatican City

The Vatican Scavi (Necropolis): Have you ever wondered where the popes go to sleep their eternal sleep? Welcome to the Scavi, home to the tombs of popes and an ancient Roman necropolis. Here, silence is more than just golden - it's mandatory!

Practical Info:

o Location: Vatican City. It's underneath St. Peter's Basilica. Literally.
o Getting There: Well, you have to walk. No Uber service is available six feet under.
o Ticket Prices: Around €13. A small price to pay for meeting the popes of yesteryears!
o Operating Hours: Tours by appointment only, so no impromptu visits.
o Recommended Time to Spend: Around 1.5 hours unless you're fascinated by the idea of resting in peace.

The Vatican Apostolic Library: It's like Hogwarts' library but without the invisibility cloak and whispering books. And with way more ancient texts and documents! Get ready to geek out!

Practical Info:

o Location: Vatican City.
o Getting There: It's a brisk walk from St. Peter's Square, assuming you're not distracted by the local gelateria.
o Ticket Prices: It's a scholarly place, but scholars need to eat, right? Inquire ahead for access permissions.

o Operating Hours: Monday to Friday, bookworm hours only. (8:45 AM to 5:15 PM)
o Recommended Time to Spend: Spend as much time as it takes to feel smarter.

The Tower of the Winds: If you've ever wanted to see a Pope's private observatory, here's your chance. This tower, built in the 1500s, was designed for Gregory XIII so he could study the heavens. No, not those heavens. The starry ones!

Practical Info:

o Location: Vatican City, of course.
o Getting There: It's a secret. Just kidding, ask for the best route from St. Peter's Square.
o Ticket Prices: It's priceless. But for you? Inquire ahead, and don't forget your Pope-coin!
o Operating Hours: Exclusive viewings only, no night-time stargazing, unfortunately.
o Recommended Time to Spend: About 1 hour should suffice unless you find a new constellation!

Key Takeaways

• **Vatican City is an integral part of Rome's identity:** Despite its status as a separate state, Vatican City is deeply intertwined with Rome's history, culture, and spiritual life. Its presence contributes significantly to the Eternal City's distinctive blend of faith, art, and power.

• **St. Peter's Basilica is an architectural masterpiece:** Combining elements of Renaissance and Baroque design, the Basilica is as much an art museum as it is a place of worship. Don't forget to check out Michelangelo's Pieta and Bernini's Baldachin!

- **The Sistine Chapel houses iconic artwork:** From Michelangelo's 'The Last Judgment' to Botticelli's 'The Trials of Moses', this Chapel is a treasure trove of art. Remember, no laughing - but it's okay if you get a neck cramp from gazing at the ceiling!

- **The Vatican Museums are a must-visit:** Spanning 54 galleries and housing a myriad of art pieces, it's a paradise for art enthusiasts. Do some cardio before you visit – these museums are not for the faint-hearted!

- **Vatican City is full of stories:** Every corner of the city tells a tale, whether it's about the Pope's escape route or the stolen Egyptian obelisk. Don't be shy about asking your guide about these fascinating stories!

- **Italian phrases are essential for a smooth visit:** From asking about opening times to seeking moments of silence, having some Italian under your belt can greatly enhance your Vatican experience.

- **Be respectful:** Remember that the Vatican is a place of deep religious significance. Be mindful of the rules, respect the silence, and dress modestly.

Chapter 5: The Piazzas of Rome: The City's Living Rooms

"The city squares are the ventricles of the city that bring it to life, not just the monuments"

- Renzo Piano

Welcome to Chapter 5, where we'll journey through Rome's vibrant piazzas - the city's living rooms, where locals debate football, nannies chase toddlers, and lovers steal kisses under the Mediterranean sun. Sure, Rome is a city of stunning architecture and millennial history, but it's the piazzas that truly bring the Eternal City to life.

Piazza Navona

Piazza Navona, where Roman life unfolds in all its chaotic glory. Here, artists argue about the merits of pastels versus oil paints, while waiters expertly dodge the clashing selfie sticks of eager tourists. The air is filled with the sweet aroma of roasting chestnuts, competing with the less poetic, but equally distinct, scent of gasoline from a passing Vespa.

The Piazza is dominated by the grandeur of the Fountain of the Four Rivers, where the gods of the Nile, Ganges, Danube, and Rio de la Plata look on at the pandemonium below them with expressions ranging from surprise to disdain. Designed by Bernini - who was definitely more of a 'fountain guy' than a 'public seating guy' - the fountain is a marvelous example of Baroque artistry.

Getting There: To visit Piazza Navona, you have several options. The easiest might be to walk, as Rome is a very walkable city and the Piazza is located in the city center.

If you prefer public transportation, you can take the following:

- o Bus: Many buses stop near Piazza Navona, including numbers 70, 81, 87, 492, and 628.
- o Metro: The closest metro stop is Barberini on Line A, but it is still a 20-minute walk from there.

Cost: The Piazza Navona is a public space, which means it's absolutely free to enter. However, your wallet might be in danger from the tantalizing cafes and souvenir shops lining the Piazza.

Operating Hours: Being an outdoor public square, Piazza Navona is open 24/7. Daytime is great for photos, but the Piazza really comes alive in the evening with street performers and musicians. It's like a constantly unfolding street party - Roman style.

Facilities: There are plenty of cafes and restaurants lining the square if you need to refuel. Public restrooms are a little scarce, but most cafes and restaurants provide restrooms for customers.

Time to Spend: You can easily spend a couple of hours exploring Piazza Navona, but the time can fly even quicker if you decide to sit at one of the terraces to people-watch and enjoy an espresso or a gelato.

Top Tip: Watch out for the crowd-drawing performances of street artists and entertainers, especially in the evenings. These performers are free to watch, but a small tip is always appreciated if you enjoy the show!

Piazza di Spagna and the Spanish Steps

Piazza di Spagna and the famous Spanish Steps - Rome's classic hangout spot for poets, artists, and... tired tourists. You see, despite their grandeur and stunning Baroque design, the 135 steps that connect the Piazza di Spagna with the Trinità dei Monti church are, in reality, a perfect spot for a breather after a long day of sightseeing.

And don't forget the Piazza itself, a vibrant square named after the Spanish Embassy to the Holy See. Now, you might be thinking, "Wait a minute, we're in Rome, why are these steps 'Spanish'?". Well, in the 17th century, the area was considered Spanish territory. So, in the spirit of good neighborliness, the Romans decided to keep the name. Trust me, it's less confusing than trying to pronounce 'Piazza di Trinità dei Monti' after a glass of wine or two!

Getting There: The easiest way to reach Piazza di Spagna and the Spanish Steps is by taking the Rome Metro Line A and getting off at Spagna station. As you exit the station, the magnificent Steps are just a short stroll away.

Operating Hours: The Piazza and the Steps are public spaces open 24/7. However, for the best experience and photos, come early morning or late evening to avoid the crowds. The afternoon can get quite busy, so be prepared for a bustling scene.

Tours: While it's perfectly fine to visit the Piazza and Steps independently, joining a guided tour could add context and enrich your experience. Numerous walking tours cover this area, providing insights into its history, architecture, and famous visitors.

Facilities: There are plenty of cafes and gelaterias around the Piazza, perfect for grabbing a snack or drink while enjoying the views. Public restrooms can be found nearby, though they may charge a small fee.

Time to Spend: You can comfortably explore the area and rest on the Steps within an hour or two. However, do make time for some people-watching, sketching, or just soaking in the atmosphere—it's a fundamental part of the Piazza di Spagna experience!

Cost: Access to the Piazza and the Spanish Steps is completely free. However, keep some cash handy for gelato, coffee, or a meal at one of the nearby cafes.

Note: Since 2019, sitting on the Spanish Steps has been prohibited to preserve the site's integrity. So, admire, and photograph, but don't take a seat!

Piazza del Popolo

Piazza del Popolo, the grand stage for the Roman hustle and bustle. This expansive square is as versatile as a Swiss Army knife. You want to grab an espresso? Check. How about basking in the glory of stunning obelisks and fountains? Double-check. Feel like staring at two identical-looking churches and questioning your sanity? Absolutely!

Now, imagine being a pigeon at Piazza del Popolo. As a feathered observer, you'd see a crowd as diverse as a United Nations conference. There are tourists gawking at maps, locals strutting around like peacocks, street artists creating masterpieces, and of course, the pigeons—watching it all while plotting their next statue attack.

In the middle of the square stands an ancient Egyptian obelisk like a senior citizen at a techno party. Imported from Heliopolis, it's the second oldest and one of the tallest obelisks in Rome. Talk about an impressive résumé!

So, if you find yourself in Piazza del Popolo, grab a coffee (let's give gelato a break), sit back, and enjoy the square's theatrical display. And if a pigeon lands near you, remember you didn't hear the statue-plotting from me.

Getting There: Piazza del Popolo is centrally located and easy to reach. Take the Metro Line A and get off at Flaminio - Piazza del Popolo station.

Operating Hours: The square is always open, but businesses and cafés in the area generally operate from around 7 AM to 11 PM.

Amenities: There are plenty of cafés, restaurants, and shops surrounding the piazza, perfect for sipping on a coffee (or an Aperol spritz) and people-watching.

Tours: There are several guided tours of Rome that include Piazza del Popolo. Some focus on history, others on art, and a few even delve into the ghost stories and legends surrounding the square.

Restrooms: You can find public restrooms in the metro station, and most cafés and restaurants will have facilities for customers.

Time to Spend: While the piazza itself can be admired in a relatively short visit, consider taking some time to sit at a café, visit the nearby churches, or stroll along Via del Corso, one of Rome's main shopping streets, which originates from this square.

Piazza Campo de' Fiori

Ever heard of "market to moonlight"? Welcome to Piazza Campo de' Fiori, a place where you can buy fresh tomatoes at dawn and dance with them under the stars! Once the heart of Rome's commercial and political life, today it's a spot where history and hedonism coexist.

By day, the piazza is a bustling farmer's market. Just like a dramatic opera, the action unfolds early as the vendors set up their stalls. You'll find everything from blood oranges that could rival a sunset, to olives as plump as a Roman cherub's cheek. The cheese selection alone might require a separate suitcase!

And the flowers! The piazza's name translates to "field of flowers," and it certainly lives up to it. You could pick up a bouquet that's nearly as beautiful as the Roman you're trying to woo.

By night, the place switches gears. It's like a character from a Fellini film, transforming from a modest market maiden into a beguiling nocturnal nymph. Tables fill the square as people clink wine glasses under the moonlight. Music spills from the bars, mingling with laughter and spirited conversation in a perfect symphony of Roman nightlife.

Oh, and let's not forget the imposing statue of Giordano Bruno, the philosopher burned at the stake in 1600 for heresy. He stands there, staring down the Vatican, reminding everyone that Rome isn't just about la dolce vita - it's also about courage and conviction. So, come to Campo de' Fiori for the tomatoes, stay for the history, and stick around for the party! You're guaranteed a fantastic day-to-night experience.

Getting there: The Piazza is located in the Parione district, a short walk from several Rome highlights like Piazza Navona and the Pantheon. The area is well-served by buses (64, 40, 46, and others). Remember, public transportation in Rome stops around midnight.

Market Operating Hours: The market is open from Monday to Saturday, typically from dawn until 2 pm. Nightlife typically kicks off around 8 pm and can go late into the night, especially on weekends.

What to Eat and Drink: There are numerous restaurants and bars surrounding the square. Prices can be a bit higher due to the touristy location, but hunting for a gem is part of the adventure!

Facilities: While the piazza itself doesn't have public restrooms, most of the bars and restaurants do.

Time to Spend: Plan to spend a couple of hours here, especially if you're going to the market and staying for lunch or dinner.

Key Takeaways

- **Every Piazza Tells a Story:** From the artistic splendor of Piazza Navona, marked by Bernini's breathtaking fountain, to the iconic Spanish Steps at Piazza di Spagna, each piazza in Rome is steeped in history and offers a unique slice of Roman life.

- **Rome's Piazzas are the City's Living Rooms:** As we learned, piazzas aren't just beautiful public spaces, they are communal living rooms where locals sip espresso, children play, artists create, and life unfolds in the most Roman way possible.

- **Piazza Navona:** A True Roman Powerhouse: Piazza Navona, once the site of a competitive stadium, is a hub of Baroque Roman artistry and the perfect place to enjoy a leisurely stroll while embracing the lively atmosphere of street artists, musicians, and bustling terraces.

- **Step it Up at Piazza di Spagna:** Remember, the Spanish Steps aren't just for sitting! They're a monumental stairway of 135 steps, a fantastic photo-op, and a gateway to some fabulous high-end shopping.

- **Piazza del Popolo - A Piazza for the People:** Whether you're checking out the ancient Egyptian obelisk, contemplating the twin churches, or just taking a breather before your ascent to the panoramic views at the Pincio Terrace, Piazza del Popolo is an oasis of calm in the heart of Rome.

- **Rome After Dark:** Rome's piazzas are charming by day but they truly come alive at night. The lights, the people, the ambiance – it's an experience not to be missed!

- **Language is Key:** As we discovered, learning some basic Italian phrases for urban navigation and social interactions can enhance your experience greatly. Simple words and phrases can help you navigate, order food, ask for directions, and even strike up conversations with locals.

- **Time is a Flexible Concept:** In Rome, many of the piazzas remain lively and bustling well into the night. So, don't worry about strict timetables. Embrace the Italian concept of 'la dolce far niente' - the sweetness of doing nothing.

- **Roman Piazzas are Free**: Unlike many other tourist attractions, Rome's beautiful piazzas are free to enjoy. You can spend as much time as you like, soaking up the atmosphere, people-watching, or simply marveling at the beautiful architecture and fountains.

- **Stay Refreshed:** Remember to refill your water bottles at Rome's numerous public fountains – it's free, and the water is fresh and delicious!

Chapter 6: Authentic Rome – Insider Tips and Local Recommendations

"To know the city, you must venture off the beaten path and discover its hidden secrets."

- Francis Ford Coppola

Ciao, explorers of the authentic, seekers of the secret and the concealed! Prepare yourself for a journey that's as Roman as carbonara without cream, as we venture into the rabbit hole of Rome's best-kept secrets.

Why stick to the typical tourist trail when you can enjoy a panino al trippa from a street vendor in Testaccio, debate about AS Roma vs. Lazio with passionate tifosi at Stadio Olimpico, or dive into a heated discussion about the city's best pizza al taglio (spoiler alert: it's a debate without end)? This, my friends, is the Rome you won't see on Instagram.

Rome's Hidden Districts

Rome is so much more than the Pantheon, Colosseum, and Vatican. It's also Pigneto and Garbatella, neighborhoods often overlooked by tourists, which are full of character, charm, and authentic Roman experiences.

Pigneto

As Roberto, a longtime resident of Pigneto puts it, "If Rome is the Eternal City, Pigneto is its eternal bohemian heart". This urban district, once the backdrop for neorealist films, has transformed into a haven for artists, musicians, and the creatively inclined. Its labyrinthine streets are lined with colorful murals and street art that tell tales of the city's spirit.

Here's your to-do list in Pigneto: Start your day with an espresso from Bar Necci, a café that's seen Pigneto evolve over the decades. Post that, get lost in the neighborhood's grid of streets, each corner throwing up a delightful surprise. You might stumble upon a local market where the aroma of fresh produce mixes with the chatter of Romans discussing everything from politics to football. For lunch, pick a trattoria at random and order the day's special.

San Lorenzo

It may be the student district, but San Lorenzo is much more than cheap beer and pizza (though there's plenty of that, too!). With a vibrant mix of independent boutiques, bohemian cafes, and a thriving nightlife scene, it's a neighborhood where Rome's youthful energy shines.

Testaccio

Once the working-class heart of Rome, Testaccio is now a gastronome's paradise. The neighborhood has a unique topography due to Monte Testaccio, an ancient Roman dump for broken terracotta pots that has now become a vibrant nightlife spot.

"You haven't tasted Rome until you've eaten in Testaccio," claims Luca, a food blogger and Testaccio resident.

Quartiere Ebraico

Steeped in history, the Jewish Ghetto is one of Rome's most distinct neighborhoods. Despite its troubled past, today, the area stands as a testament to Roman Jewish culture, with kosher bakeries, restaurants, and historic sites such as the Synagogue and Jewish Museum.

Each neighborhood has its own personality and charm, offering unique perspectives on Roman life. So, veer off the beaten path, wander through these Roman districts, and discover the Eternal City's true spirit.

Local Markets

Campagna Amica Market

Now, let's delve into the less trodden paths. If you have ever wondered where Romans get their sumptuous fresh produce from, you must venture to the Campagna Amica Market. Located in the Circus Maximus, it's a farmer's market that takes farm-to-table quite literally. Here, you'll find only Italian-grown and produced items.

Mercato di Ponte Milvio

Next up, Ponte Milvio Market. Nestled in the heart of a thriving local neighborhood, this market is where you'll find Romans buying everything from antique furniture to vintage records. This market it's like a time capsule. Every item has a story to tell.

Nuovo Mercato Esquilino

Located near the Termini Station, Nuovo Mercato Esquilino is a global food paradise. It's like the United Nations of food markets. Want some Roman pecorino cheese? Check. Need some Indian spices? Check. Craving for some Chinese bok choy? Check.

Park Life in Rome

Parco degli Acquedotti:

Are you sick of the rush of Rome's downtown? Then Parco degli Acquedotti is your haven of peace. Consider enjoying a picnic amidst the splendor of old Roman aqueducts. There is no other location like it! Locals refer to this park as their "secret backyard," a place to get away from it all, jog with their dogs, or unwind with a good book.

Roseto Comunale:

Imagine wandering through a sea of blooming roses in the heart of Rome. Welcome to Roseto Comunale, the city's municipal rose garden. It's a visual and aromatic feast! Each spring, locals flock to the garden to take part in the annual "Premio Roma" contest, where the best rose variety of the year is chosen.

You must smell the 'Via Appia' rose. It will remind you of your grandma's garden. Don't forget to find this rose when you visit!

Navigating Rome's Trickiest Traps

Street Art Scam

In Rome's bustling tourist spots, you might encounter artists seemingly innocently displaying their artwork on the busy streets. But beware, not all is as it seems. If you accidentally step on their art, they might become hostile and demand you pay for damages. Remember, in this situation, it's best to settle the matter in front of the police. Most scammers will back off at the mention of authorities. Alternatively, if you feel safe, walk away briskly without engaging.

Friendship Bracelet Scam

This scam is prevalent near popular tourist sites. A friendly person may approach you, strike up a conversation, and offer to tie a 'free' friendship bracelet on your wrist. Once it's securely tied (and virtually impossible to remove without scissors), they'll demand payment for it. These scammers can be quite pushy and aggressive. The best course of action is to refuse the offer from the start. Remember, if a stranger is giving you something for 'free,' there's a good chance it's not really free.

Gelato Overcharge Scam

Some gelato shops near major tourist sites are known for charging exorbitant prices for their scoops. Be cautious if the prices aren't clearly displayed or if they're trying to rush you into making a choice. It's best to confirm the price before you order. Remember, a scoop of gelato shouldn't cost you more than your dinner!

Gladiator Photo Scam

Posing for a photo with a 'gladiator' outside the Colosseum can seem like a fun idea, but it can also be a quick way to lose money. These costumed individuals often demand a high fee after the photo is taken. To avoid this, always negotiate the price before the photo op.

Fake Taxi Scam

Not all taxis are created equal. Be sure to only take official white taxis with a meter. Some scammers operate unlicensed taxis and might charge you an exorbitant fee. If a taxi doesn't have an official sign and a visible meter, don't get in.

The golden rule is: if something feels off, it probably is. Trust your instincts, keep your belongings secure, and stay informed. Now that you're equipped with these scam-busting tips, you can go forth and enjoy Rome with confidence!

Rome's Alternative Art Scene

Ostiense and Tor Marancia:

For those who think art belongs solely in museums, Rome's street art scene is ready to change your mind. In districts like Ostiense and Tor Marancia, buildings become canvases, and creativity literally spills onto the streets.

Strolling around Ostiense is like entering an open-air gallery. A local artist, Fabrizio, described it: "Here, we breathe art. It's our form of expression. Look at that wall! That's not just graffiti; it's a dialogue with the city."

Tor Marancia, a once overlooked residential area, has reinvented itself into an outdoor museum. Locals take pride in the vibrant murals that tell stories of their neighborhood.

Mattatoio:

Meet Rome's beating heart of contemporary art: the Mattatoio. This former slaughterhouse is now a vibrant space for exhibitions, performances, and workshops. Regularly, it hosts a variety of cultural events, including the popular 'Art Night', when the center stays open till late, buzzing with music, food, and of course, art.

Chapter 7: Savoring Rome: Cuisine That Tells a Story

Traditional Roman Dishes

Cacio e Pepe

Cacio e Pepe, which literally translates to "cheese and pepper," is the epitome of Roman culinary genius in its sheer simplicity and astonishing depth of flavor.

This is an absolute must-try for any food lover in Rome, a humble yet sophisticated dish that embodies the spirit of Roman cuisine - simple ingredients transformed into something extraordinary.

Allergens: Gluten (pasta), Dairy (cheese)

Savor it Here:

Flavio al Velavevodetto (Via di Monte Testaccio, 97, 00153 Roma RM, Italy) is a local favorite, known for its classic Roman dishes, including a divine Cacio e Pepe.

Trattoria Da Enzo (Via dei Vascellari, 29, 00153 Roma RM, Italy) is a small, homely place offering a fantastic Cacio e Pepe. Be sure to arrive early or make a reservation!

For a less-touristy experience, try Trattoria Perilli (Via Marmorata, 39, 00153 Roma RM, Italy). Their Cacio e Pepe is prepared table-side and delivers an authentic Roman culinary experience.

Carbonara

Few dishes symbolize the heartiness and richness of Roman cuisine like Carbonara. Made with guanciale (Italian cured pork cheek), eggs, Pecorino Romano, and a hearty sprinkling of black pepper, it's an iconic pasta dish that promises to satiate even the most ravenous appetite.

Allergens: Gluten (pasta), Eggs, Dairy (cheese)

Savor it Here:

Roscioli (Via dei Giubbonari, 21/22, 00186 Roma RM, Italy) is a deli-cum-restaurant that offers, arguably, one of the best Carbonara in Rome.

Trattoria Da Danilo (Via Petrarca, 13, 00185 Roma RM, Italy) is another great spot to savor Carbonara. This family-run trattoria is adored by locals.

Off the beaten path, Osteria Bonelli (Viale dell'Acquedotto Alessandrino, 172, 00177 Roma RM, Italy) in the Torpignattara neighborhood, serves an exceptional Carbonara and is favored by Romans.

Supplì

A beloved Roman street food, Supplì are fried rice balls that make for a perfect on-the-go snack or appetizer. The golden, crispy breadcrumb coating gives way to a lusciously gooey mozzarella center, enveloped by flavorful tomato rice. Each bite is a delightful contrast of textures and a celebration of straightforward, homely flavors.

Allergens: Gluten (breadcrumbs), Dairy (cheese)

Savor it here:

Supplizio (Via dei Banchi Vecchi, 143, 00186 Roma RM, Italy) specializes in Supplì and other fried goodies. Their classic Supplì is a must-try.

Pizzarium (Via della Meloria, 43, 00136 Roma RM, Italy) by Gabriele Bonci, though famous for its pizza, also serves outstanding Supplì.

For a local gem, venture to I Supplì (Via di San Francesco a Ripa, 137, 00153 Roma RM, Italy) in Trastevere, a take-away spot loved by locals for its delicious Supplì.

Saltimbocca alla Romana

When it comes to Roman cuisine, the magic lies in its simplicity and the quality of ingredients, and Saltimbocca alla Romana is no exception. A classic Roman main course, Saltimbocca, literally translates to 'jump in the mouth,' and that's exactly what this dish aims to do with its flavors!

Allergens: None

Savor it here:

• Trattoria Al Moro (Vicolo delle Bollette, 13, 00187 Roma RM, Italy) serves an exquisite version of Saltimbocca.

• Da Enzo al 29 (Via dei Vascellari, 29, 00153 Roma RM, Italy) in Trastevere is also well-known for this traditional dish.

Maritozzo

Maritozzo is a sweet treat, a traditional Roman pastry that's typically enjoyed for breakfast or a snack. These fluffy, sweet buns are slit open and generously filled with fresh whipped cream, creating a delightful contrast between the lightly sweetened dough and the rich cream.

Allergens: Gluten (wheat flour), Dairy (cream)

Savor it here:

• Roscioli (Piazza Benedetto Cairoli, 16, 00186 Roma RM, Italy) is a bakery renowned for their Maritozzi.

• Regoli (Via dello Statuto, 60, 00185 Roma RM, Italy), a pastry shop in business for over 100 years, serves some of the best Maritozzi in town.

Fiori di Zucca

Fiori di Zucca, or zucchini flowers, are a quintessential Roman appetizer. These delicate blossoms are often stuffed with mozzarella and anchovies, then lightly battered and fried until crispy. The result is a melt-in-your-mouth treat with a lovely contrast of textures and flavors.

Allergens: Gluten (wheat flour), Dairy (cheese), Fish (anchovies)

Savor it here:

• Pizzeria Baffetto (Via del Governo Vecchio, 114, 00186 Roma RM, Italy) serves delightful Fiori di Zucca as a starter.

• Da Cesare al Casaletto (Via del Casaletto, 45, 00151 Roma RM, Italy) is loved by locals for their crispy Fiori di Zucca.

Bucatini all'Amatriciana

Bucatini all'Amatriciana is a pasta dish that holds a special place in Roman hearts and stomachs. The dish is traditionally made with

Bucatini, a thick, hollow spaghetti-like pasta, tossed in a robust sauce made from guanciale (pork cheek), Pecorino cheese, and tomatoes.

Allergens: Gluten (pasta), Dairy (cheese)

Savor it here:

• Da Felice (Via Mastro Giorgio, 29, 00153 Roma RM, Italy) is a Roman institution, well-known for their superb Amatriciana.

• Trattoria Da Danilo (Via Petrarca, 13, 00185 Roma RM, Italy) serves a stellar version that's beloved by locals.

Carciufi alla Romana

Artichokes may not be the first thing that comes to mind when you think of Roman cuisine, but Carciofi alla Romana, or Roman-style artichokes, are a culinary experience you can't miss.

Allergens: None

Savor it here:

• Da Enzo al 29 (Via dei Vascellari, 29, 00153 Roma RM, Italy) is famous for its delicious artichokes.

• Il Sanlorenzo (Via dei Chiavari, 4/5, 00186 Roma RM, Italy) also serves a delightful Carciofi alla Romana.

Tiramisu

This heavenly concoction of ladyfingers soaked in coffee and a boozy mixture, layered with a rich mascarpone cream, and dusted with cocoa powder, offers a wonderful medley of flavors - bitter, sweet, creamy, and boozy all at once.

Allergens: Gluten (ladyfingers), Dairy (mascarpone), Eggs

Savor it here:

• Bar del Fico (Piazza del Fico, 26, 00186 Roma RM, Italy) offers a scrumptious Tiramisu that's a local favorite.

• Pompi (Via della Croce, 82, 00187 Roma RM, Italy) is known as the 'King of Tiramisu' and for good reason!

Trippa alla Romana

Trippa alla Romana, or Roman-style tripe, might sound daunting to the uninitiated, but this dish is a flavor powerhouse. Tripe, the lining of a cow's stomach, is slow-cooked until tender in a rich tomato sauce with mint and Pecorino cheese.

Allergens: Dairy (cheese)

Savor it here:

• Checco er Carrettiere (Via Benedetta, 10, 00153 Roma RM, Italy) serves a beautiful Trippa alla Romana, and it's a local favorite.

• Osteria Bonelli (Viale dell'Acquedotto Alessandrino, 172, 00173 Roma RM, Italy) is a bit out of the way but worth the journey for their trip.

Pajata

Pajata is a dish for the adventurous foodies, a traditional Roman recipe that uses the intestines of an unweaned calf, with the milk still inside acting as a natural, sweet-savory sauce.

Allergens: Gluten (pasta), Dairy (milk)

Savor it here:

• Perilli a Testaccio (Via Marmorata, 39, 00153 Roma RM, Italy) has been serving traditional Roman cuisine, including Pajata, since 1911.

• Da Enzo al 29 (Via dei Vascellari, 29, 00153 Roma RM, Italy) also offers a well-prepared version of Pajata.

Decoding Food and Wine Pairings in Rome

Alright gastronomads, let's delve into the harmonic world of Italian food and wine, where every meal is a symphony of flavors waiting to be conducted!

- Pasta & Sangiovese: Pasta dishes with hearty, tomato-based sauces like spaghetti alla carbonara or amatriciana pair beautifully with a Sangiovese. The high acidity and medium-bodied nature of this wine make it a pasta's best friend.

- Seafood & Vermentino: When you're digging into a delectable dish of Fritto Misto (mixed fried seafood), you'll want to have a glass of Vermentino by your side. This crisp, light-bodied white wine with its citrusy undertones complements seafood without overpowering it.

- Pizza & Barbera: Barbera, an everyday Italian red, with its fruity flavors and low tannins, is a match made in pizza heaven. Whether it's a classic Margherita or a loaded Capricciosa, Barbera will hold its own.

- Risotto & Pinot Grigio: Creamy risotto dishes find a delightful partner in Pinot Grigio. Its light and bright character helps balance the richness of the risotto.

- Beef & Super Tuscan: Tuck into a succulent Bistecca alla Fiorentina (Tuscan T-bone steak) with a robust Super Tuscan wine. The bold flavors of the wine are a great match for the strong, rich flavors of the steak.

- Gelato & Moscato d'Asti: For dessert, indulge in your favorite gelato flavor paired with a glass of lightly sparkling, sweet Moscato d'Asti. The wine's light fizz and aromatic bouquet make it the perfect partner for sweet treats.

Key Takeaways

- Carbonara: Don't ask for cream in your Carbonara when in Rome – the locals might disown you! Remember, the creaminess comes from the magic blend of eggs and Pecorino Romano.

- Maritozzo: This sweet bun isn't just for breakfast anymore! Many Romans enjoy it as a mid-morning snack, perfect with a cup of coffee.

- Saltimbocca alla Romana: The name of this dish means "jump in the mouth" in Italian. Try it, and you'll understand why – the flavors literally leap off the plate!

- Fiori di Zucca: Fried zucchini flowers are the Roman equivalent of potato chips - once you start eating them, you just can't stop. Be warned, they're addictive!

- Supplì: This crispy, gooey delight is Rome's answer to fast food. And you thought fast food couldn't be classy!

- Cacio e Pepe: Think pasta can't be a revelation? Wait till you try Cacio e Pepe – it's a Roman romance in every bite.

- Bucatini all'Amatriciana: Remember, it's not just pasta, it's Bucatini. Thicker, heartier, and just the right vehicle for the tangy, porky Amatriciana sauce.

- Carciofi alla Romana: Artichokes may seem high maintenance, but Romans know their worth. This dish will make you rethink all your vegetable preferences.

- Tiramisu: Literal translation – "pick me up". After a bite, you'll realize it's not just a dessert, it's a mood-lifter.

- Trippa alla Romana: Tripe might not be your go-to, but Rome isn't about playing it safe. This dish is a textural surprise - tender tripe in a robust tomato sauce.

- Pajata: Veal intestines never tasted this good. Remember, when in Rome, do as the Romans do. And the Romans? They love Pajata.

Chapter 8: Artistic Rome: A Paradise for Art Lovers

"Rome is the city of echoes, the city of illusions, and the city of yearning."

- Giotto di Bondone

Brace yourself, dear reader, as we're about to turn a new page (quite literally). Say goodbye to your food coma because Rome's artistic splendors are going to jolt you awake. This isn't just a chapter; it's a palette of stories painted with history, culture, and infinite talent. Hold onto your gelato, folks, because Rome is about to bare its artsy soul! Prepare for some major 'frame drops'!

Capitoline Museums

It's a constellation of art and history, located smack dab in the middle of Rome. The Capitoline Museums are a grand buffet of culture, seasoned with gorgeous sculptures, garnished with ancient artifacts, and served on the platter of a centuries-old palace.

Practical Info:

- o Location: Piazza del Campidoglio, 1, 00186 Roma RM, Italy
- o Getting There: A short stroll from the Colosseo metro station will take you right to the museums.
- o Ticket Prices: Shell out just €16 for an adult ticket to this cornucopia of culture.
- o Operating Hours: Available for your art cravings from 9.30 am to 7.30 pm, every day except on Mondays.

- o Recommended Time to Spend: At least 3-4 hours should suffice, but feel free to overstay, the art won't mind!

Borghese Gallery

If you're expecting a sleepy gallery, think again. This isn't just a museum; it's a villa that houses an art collection that could make Mona Lisa blush. The Borghese Gallery is where Bernini, Caravaggio, and Titian rock the Roman art scene.

Practical Info:

- o Location: Piazzale Scipione Borghese, 5, 00197 Roma RM, Italy
- o Getting There: Jump on bus 910 from Termini and hop off at the Borghese Gallery.
- o Ticket Prices: For €27, you're invited to this epic art party. Just remember to book in advance!
- o Operating Hours: The Gallery opens its doors from 9 am to 7 pm, Tuesdays through Sundays.
- o Recommended Time to Spend: To truly savor the art feast, reserve around 2-3 hours.

The National Museum of Rome

This one's for all the history buffs out there. The National Museum of Rome is a four-course meal of cultural richness, serving everything from prehistoric relics to the Roman Empire's coins.

Practical Info:

- o Location: Via della Salara Vecchia, 5/6, 00186 Roma RM, Italy
- o Getting There: Nestled in the city center, it's a breezy walk from the Repubblica metro station.

- Ticket Prices: Regular tickets go for €12, and it's a steal for the amount of history you're getting!
- Operating Hours: Open every day from 9 am to 7:45 pm, except Mondays.
- Recommended Time to Spend: To time-travel properly, block out around 2-3 hours on your schedule.

Centrale Montemartini Museum

Shove aside the mainstream museums and stride into a steampunk haven! Centrale Montemartini Museum is where art marries industry, and they lived happily ever after. An old power plant transformed into an art museum, it displays Greek and Roman statues against the backdrop of imposing machinery.

Practical Info:

- Location: Via Ostiense, 106, 00154 Roma RM, Italy
- Getting There: The easiest way is to hop on metro line B and get off at Garbatella.
- Ticket Prices: Adults pay €10, but the sheer awe is absolutely priceless.
- Operating Hours: Open from 9 am to 7 pm, Tuesdays through Sundays.
- Recommended Time to Spend: Devote at least 2 hours to truly appreciate this clash of epochs.

Museum of the Walls

If walls could talk, right? In Rome, they actually do! The Museum of the Walls showcases the imposing Aurelian Walls, Rome's ancient city defenses. Walk along the ramparts, ascend the towers, and let the views sweep you off your feet.

Practical Info:

- o Location: Via di Porta San Sebastiano, 18, 00179 Roma RM, Italy
- o Getting There: Take bus 118 from Circo Massimo and get off at Porta S. Sebastiano/Museo delle Mura.
- o Ticket Prices: A mere €5 gets you up close and personal with Rome's battlements.
- o Operating Hours: Open from 9 am to 2 pm, Tuesdays through Sundays.
- o Recommended Time to Spend: Give yourself about 1-2 hours to journey back to Rome's fortification days.

The Magic Door of Rome (Alchemical Door)

No, it's not a new Harry Potter book. The Magic Door of Rome is an enigmatic monument nestled in the Piazza Vittorio. Its cryptic symbols and mysterious inscriptions make it a magnet for lovers of the esoteric. The journey to understanding its secrets might be arduous, but who can resist a good magical mystery?

Practical Info:

Location: Piazza Vittorio Emanuele II, 00185 Roma RM, Italy

Getting There: It's a short walk from the Vittorio Emanuele metro station.

Ticket Prices: Gawk and guess for free, deciphering its mysteries is the only price.

Operating Hours: Always available for your wonderment.

Recommended Time to Spend: Spend around an hour, but feel free to stay longer if you're cracking the code.

The Art of Savoring Rome's Masterpieces

In Rome, the city of la dolce vita, savoring art is akin to savoring a dish at a Michelin-starred restaurant - it's not meant to be rushed. Here's your guide on how to fully appreciate the artistic banquet that Rome offers:

- Patience, Young Padawan: Forget the concept of time when you step into an art museum or gallery. Art needs time to reveal itself, its stories, and its secrets. So, don't just 'see' the art - 'experience' it.

- Quality over Quantity: Don't aim to tick off every exhibit in the museum. It's okay to miss a few lesser-known works if it means you can spend quality time appreciating the masterpieces.

- Savor Solo Moments: Go off the group tour track and spend time with the pieces that truly move you. You might not get the same thrill from a crowded Mona Lisa as you would from a less-known Caravaggio in a quiet corner.

- Reflection is Key: After taking in a piece of art, find a quiet spot in the museum (like a bench or a coffee shop) to reflect on what you saw, what it made you feel, and what it means to you.

- Guides are Gold: If possible, hire a local guide or pick up an audio guide. Their insights can deepen your understanding and appreciation of the art you're seeing.

- Sketch, Don't Snap: Instead of snapping quick photos, try sketching the artwork or writing down your thoughts about it. This will help you remember the pieces in a more personal and meaningful way.

- Stay Curious: Don't be afraid to ask questions, whether to guides, museum staff, or fellow visitors. There's no such thing as a 'stupid' question in the world of art.

Remember, viewing art is not a race; it's a journey of exploration and discovery. So, slow down, breathe in the magnificence of the Roman art scene, and let your soul be touched by the timeless stories that each piece unfolds. Because in Rome, art is not just something you see, it's something you live!

Key Takeaways

- Romans don't just display art, they live in it. If you're planning to visit Rome, pack a pair of artistically-inclined spectacles!

- You haven't experienced art until you've walked through a centuries-old palace filled with sculptures and ancient artifacts - Capitoline Museums, we're looking at you!

- Always thought art was a bit snoozy? A visit to the Borghese Gallery will convince you otherwise - and you get to stroll through a garden that is art itself!

- The National Museum of Rome isn't just for history buffs. It's a journey from prehistoric relics to the Roman Empire's coins. Who knew history could be so captivating?

- If you thought Aphrodite and a diesel engine were worlds apart, wait till you visit the Centrale Montemartini Museum. It's a mesmerizing marriage of art and industry!

- Turns out, walls can talk! Or at least, Rome's Aurelian Walls can. A stroll along the Museum of the Walls is a journey through Rome's military history.

- Harry Potter fans, rejoice! The Magic Door of Rome isn't Diagon Alley, but it's an enigmatic monument full of cryptic symbols and mysterious inscriptions. Who needs magic wands when you've got magical mysteries?

And that's a wrap on our whirlwind tour of Rome's artistic treasures. Buckle up, because in the next chapter, we're taking you on a journey through the city's distinctive neighborhoods, public gardens, and breathtaking city views.

Chapter 9: Preparing for Your Italian Adventure

"The world is a book, and those who do not travel read only one page."

- Saint Augustine

All aboard the plane to Rome! But wait, what's that? An overflowing suitcase and a list of unending prep? Fear not, fellow traveler, for we've got your back. In this chapter, we turn the arduous task of packing into a delightful game of "Smart, Chic, and Oh So Italian!" Grab your pen and paper, and buckle up, because we're about to embark on the funniest crash course in efficient, stylish, and oh-so-Roman holiday preparation!

Getting Ready: Packing Essentials

When it comes to packing for your Roman adventure, we've got two words for you: Smart and Chic. You've got to outsmart the weather, the walking, and the potential weight of your suitcase while still looking photo-ready for those iconic Roman backdrops. Easy, right? Not to worry, dear globetrotter. Let's break it down.

Clothing: Rome is a city of style. That doesn't mean you need to strut around in high fashion ensembles but think comfortable yet chic. Remember, Italians love to dress up a little, even when they're going to the grocery store.

Spring/Summer: Think light. Breathable fabrics, sunglasses, a hat for the sun, and don't forget that swimsuit for a potential beach day!

Fall/Winter: Layer up! Bring a good jacket, scarves, gloves, and warm socks. An umbrella or raincoat might also come in handy.

Footwear: Cobblestones are Rome's favorite street décor. Pretty to look at, but a little tricky underfoot. Bring comfortable walking shoes. Also, pack a pair of nicer shoes for a swanky dinner or opera night.

Toiletries: The usual suspects - toothbrush, toothpaste, shampoo, conditioner, etc. If you're particular about brands, bring travel-sized versions from home. Rome's pharmacies (Farmacia) are well stocked if you forget anything.

Electronics: Don't forget your phone, charger, power bank, and travel adapter for Italian sockets. A good ebook reader or travel guide can be handy for those long waits in line at the museums.

Documents: Passport, travel documents, credit cards, and cash - Keep these safe and have copies stored elsewhere.

Snacks: Long lines can mean long waits. A small snack can be a lifesaver, plus, who doesn't love a little mid-morning chocolate treat? Remember, Rome might have plenty of food, but it's not a fan of eating on the go.

Staying Connected - Local SIM Cards & Portable Wi-Fi

Before you land in Rome, it's good to know how you'll be staying connected. Roaming charges can be a nasty surprise, so consider getting a local SIM card upon arrival. Providers such as TIM, Vodafone, and Wind have stores all over Rome and offer good deals for tourists. If you're a group or a family, consider getting a portable Wi-Fi device (like Tep Wireless or Skyroam). These little gadgets can connect multiple devices to the Internet wherever you are.

Health & Safety - International Health Insurance and Local Health Apps

It's always good to have a safety net. Ensure you have international health insurance that can cover any potential medical costs. Also, it can be helpful to download the 'Pronto Soccorso' app. It shows the wait times at various emergency rooms in Rome.

Power Up - Power Banks and Universal Adapters

Rome is packed with Instagrammable moments. Don't let your device die on you just as you're about to snap the perfect picture at the Colosseum. Invest in a reliable power bank. Also, remember that Italy uses Type L power outlets, so bring a universal adapter.

Remember, packing smart is as crucial as packing light. So, have your essentials covered, stay connected, and prepare for any eventuality. Rome is calling, and you must go, but next, we'll tell you when you should go. Yes, we're diving into the seasons and when it's best to visit the Eternal City!

Understanding the Roman Calendar: Best Time to Visit

1. Spring (March to June): Spring is probably the best time to visit Rome. The weather is pleasantly warm, and the city is in full bloom, literally and metaphorically. The tourist crowds are yet to reach their summer peak, giving you some breathing space at popular attractions. Plus, there's Easter. Rome during Easter is a spectacle in itself, with many religious processions and services.

2. Summer (June to August): While the weather is sunny and warm, summer in Rome can be quite intense, with

temperatures often soaring above 30°C (86°F). This is also peak tourist season, so expect large crowds, especially at major sites like the Colosseum and the Vatican. On the bright side, there's gelato. Lots and lots of delicious gelato to keep you cool.

3. Autumn (September to November): Autumn is like spring's mirror image. The weather is mild, the summer crowds are thinning, and the city is painted in warm autumn hues. This is also a great time to enjoy Rome's parks and outdoor spaces.

4. Winter (December to February): Winters in Rome are quite mild compared to many other European cities. Plus, you'll have the city's iconic sites practically to yourself. The downside is shorter days and fewer hours of sunshine. But then, there's Christmas. Rome goes all out during the festive season, and the city is beautifully lit and decorated.

Building Your Itinerary: Planning Your Days in Rome

One of the biggest mistakes people make when visiting Rome? Trying to squeeze 3,000 years of history into a two-day visit. Trust me, you don't want to do that. Remember, Rome wasn't built in a day, so don't try to conquer it in one, either.

Here are some tried-and-true tips for building an itinerary that lets you enjoy Rome without running yourself ragged.

Know your interests: Rome has something for everyone. History buffs, foodies, fashionistas, art lovers - this city caters to every kind of traveler. So, ask yourself what interests you the most. Are you passionate about ancient history? Can't resist a good shopping spree? Do you drool over Italian cuisine? This will help you prioritize your 'must-see' list.

1. **Plan but be flexible:** Rome is full of surprises. You never know when you'll stumble upon a charming cafe or a street performance that catches your eye. So, while it's important to have a plan, don't stick to it too rigidly. Allow some wiggle room for spontaneous moments of Roman magic.

2. **Balance your days:** A common pitfall is trying to pack too much into a single day. Yes, Rome has a lot to offer, but that doesn't mean you have to see it all at once. Aim to visit one major attraction per day, mixed in with smaller sites, leisurely meals, and rest periods. Remember, travel is a marathon, not a sprint.

3. **Take advantage of late opening hours:** Some sites, like the Vatican Museums and the Colosseum, have late opening hours on certain days. These are often less crowded and offer a different ambiance.

4. **Factor in downtime:** Don't underestimate the value of a well-timed gelato break or a leisurely walk through a park. Rome is as much about the dolce far niente (sweet doing nothing) as it is about sightseeing.

5. **Neighborhood Navigation:** Like a flavorful antipasto platter, Rome is best enjoyed one bite at a time. When charting your journey, group attractions that are neighbors to optimize

your time. This way, you don't end up crisscrossing the city like a confused pigeon!

6. VIP or Bust: No one likes waiting in lines, especially under the Roman sun. Think of skip-the-line or guided tour tickets as your VIP pass to history, minus the velvet rope. A few extra euros can save you from the boredom of queues and enrich your experience with insights from those who know Rome inside and out.

7. Time It Right: Rome's beauty shines differently throughout the day. Make the most of early mornings or late evenings when iconic sites bask in a softer glow and hum with fewer people. You might not have the moonlight serenade to yourself, but it's the closest you'll get!

8. Post-It Plan: Sometimes, the old ways are the best ways! Grab a city map, some colored markers, and Post-Its. Write your points of interest on separate notes and stick them in their corresponding locations. This visual approach helps you see clusters of activities and plan efficient routes. Don't worry if it looks like a toddler's art project. It's your ultimate guide to Rome!

9. Theme Days: Make each day of your trip a unique story. Have a "History Day" filled with ancient ruins, a "Foodie Day" packed with culinary explorations, or a "Relaxation Day" where you do nothing but soak up the la dolce vita. This way, each day becomes an adventure of its own!

10. Listen to the Locals: Who knows a city better than the ones living in it? Don't shy away from asking locals for their advice – favorite restaurants, lesser-known museums, or

secret sunset spots. You may just discover Rome's best-kept secrets and add an unplanned gem to your itinerary.

11. The Piazza Pause: Rome is scattered with beautiful piazzas, perfect for people-watching, a quick bite, or just a breather. Plan your itinerary such that every few hours, you have a charming piazza on your path to rest your feet and soak in the city vibes. Remember, in Rome, every moment is an opportunity to savor la dolce vita.

Flight to Rome: Choosing the Right Airline

Who knew that choosing a flight could be as complex as choosing a gelato flavor in Rome? Well, don't worry, we're here to make it as painless as possible. The key is to find a balance between cost, comfort, and convenience.

1. Research Airlines: Not all airlines are created equal. Some may offer cheaper fares, while others may excel in service and comfort. Look at customer reviews and safety ratings to make an informed decision. Flagship carriers like Alitalia have direct flights from many major cities, while budget airlines like Ryanair might have cheaper fares but fewer services and more layovers.

2. Beware of Hidden Fees: With the rise of budget airlines, it's important to read the fine print. What might seem like a great deal at first could quickly become expensive with added baggage fees, seat selection charges, and meal costs. Make sure you're comparing apples to apples when looking at different fares.

3. Consider Layovers: Sometimes, flights with layovers can be cheaper than direct flights. However, they also increase travel time and the risk of delays or lost luggage. If you're considering a flight with a layover, check the duration and the airport. A seven-hour layover in Reykjavik might be a fun chance to explore, but a two-hour layover in a sprawling airport like JFK might be cutting it close.

4. Timing is Everything: Prices can vary significantly depending on the time of day, the day of the week, and how far in advance you book. Generally, mid-week flights are cheaper than weekend flights, and booking at least three months in advance can save you some money. Websites like Skyscanner or Google Flights can help you compare prices and choose the most economical times to fly.

5. Join the Club: Many airlines have rewards programs that offer free or discounted flights, upgrades, and other perks. If you travel frequently, it's worth signing up. Some airlines also offer co-branded credit cards with sign-up bonuses that can cover part or all of a flight to Rome.

Key Takeaways

- Packing Essentials: Remember the mantra: smart and chic. Dress appropriately for the season, don't underestimate the cobblestone streets, and keep room for snacks! Also, keep your documents safe and copies stored elsewhere.

- Staying Connected: Avoid roaming charges by getting a local SIM card from providers like TIM, Vodafone, and Wind. If traveling as a group, a portable Wi-Fi device could be a smart investment.

- Health & Safety: International health insurance is a must for any travel abroad. Also, it's a good idea to download the 'Pronto Soccorso' app for info on wait times at various emergency rooms in Rome.

- Power Up: Rome is packed with Instagram-worthy moments, so don't let your device die just when you've lined up the perfect shot. Bring a reliable power bank and a universal adapter for Italian sockets.

- Understanding the Roman Calendar: Rome is beautiful all year round, but each season has its unique charm. Spring and Autumn are milder and less crowded, while Summer is perfect for gelato lovers, and Winter offers a festive atmosphere.

- Building Your Itinerary: Prioritize according to your interests, balance your days with major and minor attractions, take advantage of late opening hours, and always factor in downtime.

- Choosing the Right Airline: Not all airlines are created equal. Research thoroughly, beware of hidden fees, consider the pros and cons of layovers, and be smart about when to book. Joining airline reward programs can also lead to significant savings.

Conclusion

And there we have it, amici! We stand at the brink of our Roman expedition. Over the course of this guide, we have walked through the Roman cobblestone streets, experienced its profound culture, and even got a taste of its delightful language and flavors. But keep in mind, this isn't the end. It's only the beginning of your very own Italian adventure.

What have we tucked away in your Roman travel kit?

- **Historic Attractions and Secret Spots:** Rome, an eternal enigma, is a magnificent blend of iconic landmarks and less-traveled nooks. We've acquainted you not only with the Colosseum and St. Peter's Basilica but also with the quieter lanes that lead to hidden gems like the gardens of Villa Borghese and the mesmerizing view from the Aventine Keyhole.

- **Cultural Insights and Etiquette:** You've received a glimpse into the Roman psyche, their food culture, their traditional etiquettes, and their unwritten rules. This knowledge enables you to blend in effortlessly with the locals and navigate the city with an insider's savvy.

- **A Personalized Itinerary for Your Roman Adventure:** You're now equipped with a roadmap to plan an unforgettable Roman adventure that aligns with your interests, budget, and, importantly, your Italian language learning goals.

- **Digital Tools to Enhance Your Experience:** Our inclusion of custom Google Maps for each chapter, showcasing each location discussed, promises to make your journey through Rome smooth and immersive. Moreover, our Italian learning guides are there to help you communicate and connect on a deeper level with the heart of Italy - its people.

So, are you ready? It's time to embark on your Roman adventure with a piece of newfound knowledge, confidence, and excitement. Rome awaits you, with its millennia-old ruins, its charming piazzas, and its beautiful language. Buon viaggio, amici, and here's to the unforgettable experiences that await you in the eternal city of Rome!

Book 2

Florence Travel Guide

Explore to Win

Introduction

"A man who has not been in Italy is always conscious of an inferiority."

- Samuel Johnson

Ready to hack your way into the hidden Florence, the one that's off-limits to your garden-variety globetrotter? Because if you're eyeing this book, you're not the sort to be herded through tourist traps. Nope, you're the real deal—a culture vulture hungry for the Florence that's been hiding in plain sight.

Hold up, this isn't your grandma's travel guide, and Florence is not a one-hit-wonder city that you can sum up with a quick visit to the Duomo. Nope, we're going off-script, past the selfie sticks, and right into the soul of this Italian masterpiece. We're talking unsung eateries where every pasta swirl captures centuries of culinary artistry, and quiet piazzas that ditch the fanfare but pack a cultural punch.

Why should you bookmark Florence as your next dream destination? Think of it as the Swiss Army knife of travel experiences. It's got a bit of everything—food that will make your taste buds dance the Tarantella, art that will have you questioning your life choices (in a good way), and history that's far juicier than any soap opera.

Convinced yet? This guide is your backstage pass to Florence, granting you access to places Google Maps won't show and experiences TripAdvisor can't rate. We'll journey from secret Medici passageways to subterranean wine cellars that will make you forget Napa Valley even exists.

Who am I to take you on this tour? Let's just say I've walked these streets, taken notes, and sampled enough gelato to consider myself somewhat of an aficionado. We're talking serious street cred, combined with a knack for unearthing experiences that most travelers overlook.

Intrigued? Good, because we're not stopping at mere sightseeing. This guide will catapult you into local life as if you've been bestowed a Florentine passport. Fancy a little mystery? We're going to unravel Florence's hidden gems that even some locals might not know about. The tiny boutiques, the mouthwatering food stalls, the unexpected art installations—get ready to experience them all.

Perhaps you've been frustrated by travel guides in the past. The tourist traps, the "must-sees" that are anything but, and oh, the clichés! "Don't forget to toss a coin in the Trevi Fountain for good luck!" How about we toss out the clichés instead? Here, every tip and trick is finely tuned to offer a bespoke travel experience, curated just for you.

And yes, we'll talk about wine and pasta. But not just any wine or pasta. I'm talking about that tucked-away vineyard where each grape bursts with history, or that family-owned trattoria where the pasta recipe has been guarded like a national treasure.

Now, you might wonder how we're going to cram all of Florence's splendors into one guide. You'll skip the long lines of common knowledge and head straight to the good stuff. Ever heard of secret bakeries that operate only in the dead of night, serving up fresh pastries to those in the know? Yep, you'll find out how to score an invite.

Sure, Florence is a city for romantics. But let's ditch the notion that you need to be head-over-heels in love to enjoy a moonlit stroll along the Arno River. Whether you're a solo adventurer, a history buff, or a family of explorers, Florence has a charm that's multi-faceted and inclusive.

And for those worrying about language barriers, relax. By the end of this guide, you'll have pocketed a few Italian phrases that go beyond the staple "Ciao" and "Grazie." Picture yourself haggling over leather goods in flawless Italian or raising your wine glass while uttering a toast that impresses your Florentine hosts. That's the sort of savvy we're aiming for.

Why stay confined to virtual scrolling when you could be living the Florentine dream? Your Instagram feed might offer you pixels, but Florence serves up a full, live-action panorama that's waiting just for you.

So, what's holding you back? Flip to the next chapter. We're about to explore Florence's epic past—a tale of art, ingenuity, and power struggles that even Hollywood couldn't dream up. Trust me, you don't want to miss this.

Chapter 1: Florence - The Cradle of the Renaissance

"Everything about Florence seems to be colored with a mild violet, like diluted wine."

-Henry James

Buckle up, because Florence's past is about as tame as a caffeinated squirrel at a nut festival. This isn't a city that read the "How to Make History" handbook and thought, "Eh, seems like too much work." Nope, Florence wrote the book, tossed it into the Arno River, and started sculpting, painting, and feuding its way into legend.

So, you think the Renaissance is all lofty sonnets and dusty old paintings? Think again! Florence's version of the Renaissance is like your favorite movie, but with plot twists that make Shakespeare look like a rom-com writer. Let's hop in our proverbial DeLorean and see what made this city the epicenter of *'OMG, did that just happen?'* Ready? Onward!

Italy in a Nutshell

Let's pull the camera back for a second to take in the whole glorious Italian boot, a nation that's as varied as the herbs in your Nonna's spice rack. From the Alps in the north to the Mediterranean blues down south in Sicily, Italy offers a tapestry of experiences that could take lifetimes to unravel.

But let's zoom in on Florence, nestled in the rolling hills of Tuscany. Think of Florence as the basil in your Italian pesto; it's essential, aromatic, and brings a whole lot of depth to the table.

Cultural Smorgasbord

Florence is the Renaissance capital of the world, but it's also a microcosm of Italy's varied cultural landscape. Take a stroll and you'll hear snatches of the local Florentine dialect, distinct from your standard Italian, echoing in the piazzas. You'll see street performers acting out scenes from Dante's "Divine Comedy" one block away from Senegalese vendors selling African crafts.

Local Tip: Want to catch Florence's artisan vibe in action? Make a beeline for the Oltrarno district. You'll find charming workshops where you can watch artisans breathe life into wood, leather, and metal, just as they've done for centuries.

Useful Info: The Firenze Card is your golden ticket to Florence's rich array of museums without the wait. Trust me; skipping the lines at the Uffizi alone makes it worth every euro.

Why This Matters: For foodies, a visit to Mercato Centrale is a must. The ground floor offers fresh Tuscan produce, while the upper level is a gastronomic wonderland where you can dine on everything from Florentine steak to fresh sushi, encapsulating the city's blend of tradition and modernity.

Sure, Italy is diverse, but Florence is one of its brightest jewels—captivating, multi-layered, and ever intriguing. In the coming chapters, we'll dive into each of these tantalizing facets of Florentine life in more detail, so you won't just be visiting—you'll be living Florence.

The Florence You Didn't Know

We all know that Florence gave us the Renaissance, but did you know it also played a pivotal role in the Futurist movement of the early 20th century? Yep, that avant-garde, "let's shake things up" attitude wasn't just for Paris and New York.

Example: Giacomo Balla's "Street Light," housed in the lesser-visited Museo Novecento, is a masterpiece that breaks from tradition, and it's right here in Florence.

Traveler's Tip: After you've had your fill of the Renaissance at the Uffizi, take a detour to the Museo Novecento to explore how Florence continued to redefine art through the centuries.

The Unsung Heroes of Florentine Politics

Move over, Medici! Florence had its share of political rule-breakers who were overshadowed by the famous banking family but made significant contributions to modern political thought.

Example: Niccolò Machiavelli, whose cunning political strategies were penned down in "The Prince," was a civil servant in the Republic of Florence before his exile.

Why This Matters: His concepts still influence global politics today—making him a must-know for any modern globetrotter.

The Politically Charged Art Installations

Florence is politically savvy even in its contemporary art scene. Public art installations often address current political issues, blending the past and present in a unique dialogue.

Example: The "Ttzzz...F" installation in Piazza della Signoria questioned the role of political stability in an ever-changing world.

Traveler's Tip: Keep an eye out for temporary installations during your visit; they offer fresh perspectives that bring you back to present-day issues.

Meet the Celebs of Renaissance Florence

Leonardo da Vinci

Sure, you've heard of da Vinci, the man who gave us the Mona Lisa and The Last Supper. But did you know he also designed an early version of the helicopter? Florence was where young Leo cut his teeth as an apprentice in Andrea del Verrocchio's workshop.

Example: His anatomical sketches were not just art but groundbreaking contributions to medical science.

Why You Should Care: Imagine wandering through the same streets that once inspired da Vinci. In Florence, you're literally walking in the footsteps of giants.

Michelangelo

Michelangelo is famous for the David and the Sistine Chapel, but his talents didn't stop at sculpting and painting. He was also an accomplished poet and architect.

Local Tip: Instead of joining the throngs around David at the Accademia, sneak away to the Medici Chapel to appreciate Michelangelo's genius in a quieter setting.

Why This Matters: Understanding the breadth of Michelangelo's talents deepens your appreciation of every stone and brushstroke in Florence.

The Medici

You can't talk about Florence without mentioning the Medici family. But aside from their role as art patrons, they were also political game-changers who invented modern banking.

Example: Cosimo de' Medici was one of the first to offer loans in exchange for collateral, effectively creating a pawn shop.

Traveler's Tip: Visit the Medici Riccardi Palace, where you can explore rooms like the Hall of Mirrors and see a different side of their legacy.

Lesser-Known But Not to Be Overlooked

Bianca Cappello: A Venetian beauty who climbed the social ladder through a scandalous affair with Francesco I de' Medici and became a respected noblewoman. Her story tells you something about the social dynamics of the time.

Antonio Meucci: Long before Alexander Graham Bell, this Florentine inventor created an early version of the telephone. His work shows that innovation has long been in the city's DNA.

Local Customs and Etiquettes

Navigating a city like Florence means more than just knowing which bus takes you to the Uffizi Gallery. It's about blending in with the locals, not just geographically but culturally. Let's set you up for success with some unspoken rules.

The Do's:

- ✓ Greet Like a Florentine: A simple "Buongiorno" in the morning or "Buonasera" in the evening will do wonders for your street cred.

- ✓ Queue, But Make It Italian: Italians may not be known for orderly lines, but they respect a "system" of knowing who came before and after them. Get in line, but keep an eye out for your turn.

- ✓ Dress Smart: Florentines have style. You don't need to go full runway, but maybe leave the flip-flops and tank tops for the beach.

- ✓ Respect Meal Times: Don't expect to eat dinner at 6 p.m. Most restaurants don't even open for dinner until 7:30 p.m., and locals usually dine even later.

The Don'ts:

- ✓ Don't "Ciao" Too Soon: "Ciao" is casual. Stick to the formal greetings until someone says you can switch. Trust me, you'll know when.

- ✓ Don't Over-Tip: Service charge is usually included in your restaurant bill. An extra euro or two is appreciated but not required.

- ✓ No Touchy-Feely with the Produce: At markets, wait for the vendor to assist you. Touching fruits and veggies yourself is a faux pas.

- ✓ Don't Drink Cappuccino After Noon: Just don't. Locals will know you're a tourist, and somewhere, an Italian grandma will sense it and disapprove.

Seasonal Highlights

Let's talk seasons, folks! Sure, Florence is stunning year-round, but each season has its own particular flair, like the different toppings on your favorite pizza.

Spring:

Blooms & Art: Imagine Renaissance gardens coming to life. It's the perfect time for art lovers to explore open-air museums.

Why You'd Love It: Mild temperatures, fewer crowds. Great for those Instagram snaps without a thousand tourists in your shot.

Summer:

Hot & Buzzing: Yes, Florence can turn into a scorcher. But hey, more reasons to indulge in gelato, right?

Why You'd Love It: Night markets, open-air cinemas, and street festivals. This is Florence in party mode.

Autumn:

Wine & Dine: Harvest season! Think wine tours and truffle hunting.

Why You'd Love It: Fall foliage transforms the Tuscan landscape. Fewer crowds mean a more authentic experience and better dining options without the wait.

Winter:

Holiday Charm: Christmas markets and New Year's Eve festivities offer a different kind of Florence experience.

Why You'd Love It: You'll find the most sumptuous Italian comfort food during this season. Plus, fewer tourists means you can hog all the art in the Uffizi to yourself.

Local Legends or Myths

The legends and myths. The garlic to your pasta, the secret sauce of any travel experience! So, what's Florence hiding in its ancient, cobbled lanes? Let me dish out a spicy one for you.

The Tale of Dante's Hidden Portrait

You've heard of Dante Alighieri, right? The "Divine Comedy" guy. What you might not know is that inside Florence's Palazzo Vecchio, there's said to be a secret portrait of him. According to whispers, the artist Domenico di Michelino painted Dante's face hidden within the folds of a Sibyl's robe in the artwork "The Allegory of the Imprisoned Souls." Locals sometimes say that this clandestine portrait watches over the city, keeping its artistic soul alive.

Why is this cool for you? If you're planning to visit Palazzo Vecchio (which you absolutely should), now you're not just looking at art—you're on a treasure hunt. And let's be honest, who wouldn't want to discover a centuries-old Easter egg in a Renaissance masterpiece?

The Legend of Il Porcellino

Have you heard of Il Porcellino, the bronze wild boar statue near Mercato Nuovo? Touching its snout is said to bring good luck and ensure your return to Florence. What's the real hoot? It's a tradition to rub its nose and then toss a coin over your shoulder into the grate below the statue. If the coin falls through the grate, luck is on your side!

Why You Should Care: Looking for a surefire way to come back to Florence? Give Il Porcellino a pat and make your wish. Who knows? Magic could be real.

Biancone: Florence's Lucky Giant

Situated in the Loggia della Signoria, the Biancone (Big White One) is another magnet for luck. The legend is that making a wish while touching its nose will make it come true.

Why You Should Care: Think of it as your personal genie, except carved in marble. A fun little ritual before you venture deeper into Florence's wonders.

Key Takeaways

- Florence's artistic influence extends beyond the Renaissance, playing a vital role in modern art movements like Futurism.
- The city's politics were shaped not just by famous families but also by lesser-known but significant figures like Machiavelli.
- Futurist art is an overlooked aspect of Florence's cultural contributions.
- Political thought in Florence extends far beyond the Medici, influencing modern global politics.
- Leonardo da Vinci and Michelangelo were polymaths, contributing to multiple fields beyond art.
- The Medici family were not just art patrons but pioneers in modern banking and politics.
- Bianca Cappello and Antonio Meucci are examples of lesser-known figures who played significant roles in Florence's history.

- Local Customs and Etiquettes: Learn how to make a good impression and avoid faux pas, like tipping too much or ordering a cappuccino after noon.
- Seasonal Highlights: Each season in Florence offers unique experiences, from the festive vibe of summer to the culinary delights of autumn. Choose your season wisely to get the most out of your trip.
- Local Legends or Myths: Florence has intriguing tales like Dante's Hidden Portrait that add layers of mystique to the city. These stories are not just fun but offer a new way to engage with Florence's art and landmarks.

Action Steps

- ✓ **For the Art Buffs:** Ditch the tourist map. Skip the typical Uffizi Gallery route for a day and explore the Museo Novecento to dive into Futurist art.
- ✓ **For the History Enthusiasts:** Read "The Prince". Buy a copy from a local bookstore and read it while sipping espresso in a café that's been around since Machiavelli's time.
- ✓ **For the Foodies:** Instead of a touristy cooking class, arrange to cook a traditional Florentine meal with a local family. This is the best way to understand the city's culinary roots.
- ✓ **For the Politically Curious:** Visit the Palazzo Vecchio but pay special attention to the Hall of the Five Hundred. Imagine the political intrigues that took place there.
- ✓ **For Everyone:** Customize Your Route. Create a walking tour based on your unique interests. Mix and match from art to politics to food.

Ready to take your Florence adventure up a notch? In the next chapter, we're stepping away from the textbooks and diving straight into the heart-pounding, eye-widening, "can't-believe-I'm-actually-seeing-this" stuff. We're talking about unmissable attractions that you'll be bragging about for years to come. Trust me, you don't want to miss this! Onward to Chapter 2: Unmissable Attractions in Florence!

Chapter 2: Unmissable Attractions in Florence

"Through these old streets I wander dreamily; Around me Florence sweeps her busy tide of life."

-William Leighton

So, you've wrapped your head around the history and vibrant culture of Florence. Great start! Now, it's time to weave those threads of knowledge into the fabric of experience. Think Florence is all about mainstream museums and throngs of tourists? Think again! Florence hides its most captivating gems in plain sight, and with this guide, we're spilling the beans (or should I say the olives?).

From the shadowy corners of lesser-known piazzas to bustling artisanal workshops, there's so much more to Florence than meets the eye. Ready to uncover the city's best-kept secrets and iconic landmarks with a fresh perspective? Dive in, and let's get our hands delightfully dirty with Florentine wonders.

Uffizi Gallery: Art, History, and... Selfies with Botticelli?

Ever wondered where to strike your next dramatic, art-inspired pose for the 'gram? Or perhaps where you can whisper sweet nothings to Botticelli's Venus without a beach in sight? The answer is The Uffizi Gallery. Yes, Florence's pièce de résistance in the art world, where each corridor echoes with the musings of past artistic maestros.

The gallery's exterior, with its grand columns and intricate stonework, is just a teaser. Step inside, and you'll be walking into a portal where time feels elastic. Here, the atmosphere is thick with the genius of the Renaissance: vibrant colors of frescoes, delicate brush strokes on canvases, and sculptures that seem one breath away from coming to life. If art had a Mecca, the Uffizi would probably be it. And if you don't saunter through its halls, well, let's just say you're missing an audience with the rockstars of the art world.

Practicalities - Your Uffizi Toolkit:

- **How to Get There:** Located near Piazza della Signoria; a short walk from the Florence Santa Maria Novella train station.
- **What to See:** Must-sees include "The Birth of Venus" by Botticelli, "Annunciation" by Leonardo da Vinci, and "Medusa" by Caravaggio.
- **Hours:** Generally open from 8:15 am to 6:50 pm. Closed on Mondays.
- **Tickets:** It's wise to book in advance, especially during tourist season. Combination tickets can provide access to other attractions.
- **Tour or No Tour:** Guided tours offer deep dives into the art, but wandering solo lets you set your pace.
- **Refresh:** There's a rooftop café. Perfect for an espresso with a side of breathtaking views.
- **Shop:** Don't leave without browsing the gift shop for quirky art-inspired souvenirs.
- **Photography:** Allowed, but without flash. Get those selfie angles right!
- **Accessibility:** The gallery is wheelchair accessible, with available elevators.

- **Tip:** Arrive early or during the late afternoon to dodge the major crowds.

Florence Cathedral (Duomo di Firenze)

Do you ever get the urge to shout, "I can see my house from here!" from a top-tier vantage point? Well, if you're searching for that ideal spot in Florence, look no further than the iconic Duomo di Firenze. No, seriously, this isn't just any ol' cathedral. The Duomo is like that overachieving cousin who's good at everything—they tower above the competition, quite literally.

Resplendent in pink, green, and white marble, the cathedral is an opulent testament to human determination and creativity. But it's Brunelleschi's dome—the architectural crown jewel—that truly steals the show. As you scale its winding steps, each one taking you closer to the heavens, you're in for a panoramic treat that'll make your heart skip a beat... or maybe that's just the workout!

Practicalities - Your Duomo Cheat Sheet:

- **Location:** Right smack in the heart of Florence, Piazza del Duomo. You can't miss it; it's the massive, gorgeous structure photobombing your touristy snaps.
- **Must-Dos:** Climb Brunelleschi's dome for a stellar view and explore the underground Santa Reparata remains.
- **Hours:** Generally 10:00 am to 4:30 pm, but can vary. Closed on Sundays.
- **Tickets:** Various ticket options available. Consider a combo-ticket that grants access to other nearby monuments.
- **Wardrobe Tip:** Dress modestly—shoulders and knees covered, folks!
- **Footwear:** Wear comfortable shoes. Those steps aren't climbing themselves.

- **Tour Options:** Self-guided or organized tours. Audio guides are available for rent.
- **A Bit of Caution:** The climb to the top isn't for the faint-hearted. Narrow stairs and tight spaces are involved.
- **Restrooms:** Available, but bring some change.
- **Shopping:** Yes, there's a gift shop. Because what's a landmark without some souvenirs?

Ponte Vecchio

You know that drawer at home filled with mismatched jewelry, a quirky brooch, and maybe a stray earring? Ponte Vecchio is like that, but on steroids—a bridge that decided to put on some sparkle!

Jewelers, art dealers, and souvenir sellers line this iconic bridge, making it more than just a pathway across the Arno River. Built on the whims of Medici, Ponte Vecchio is history with a golden touch. And, fun fact: It's the only Florentine bridge that World War II left standing. Even wartime leaders, it seems, couldn't bear to part with its charm.

Practicalities - Your Bridge Basics:

- **Location:** Central Florence, connecting two sides of the Arno River.
- **Highlight:** Window shopping! Those jewelry stores aren't just for show.
- **Hours:** The bridge itself? Always open. Shops? Usually 10:00 am to 8:00 pm.
- **Best Time to Visit:** Early morning or sunset. Perfect lighting for that Instagram shot.
- **Nearby Attractions:** Uffizi Gallery and Palazzo Vecchio are just a stone's throw away.

- **Watch Out:** Beware of pickpockets; they love the bridge as much as you will.
- **Fun Tip:** Look for the corridor overhead; it's the secretive Vasari Corridor that once let the Medici family move unseen.

Once you're done admiring, grab a gelato nearby and enjoy the view. Just remember: while the bridge might beckon you to buy, your wallet doesn't always have to answer!

Palazzo Vecchio: Florence's Ultimate Powerhouse

Ever wanted to time-travel to the days when lords and ladies ruled, and a tweet was just a bird's song? Welcome to Palazzo Vecchio, Florence's own time machine! This fortress-turned-town-hall has witnessed dramas worthy of a Netflix series: political plots, lavish weddings, and Medici shenanigans.

Stepping inside feels like intruding on a Medici family gathering. There's a room with walls screaming tales of power and rooms whispering secrets of clandestine meetings. And the art! It's like attending a Renaissance art convention without the entrance fee.

Your Palazzo Practicalities:

- **Location:** Piazza della Signoria. You can't miss it. Literally.
- **Highlight:** The Salone dei Cinquecento. It's grandeur overload.
- **Hours:** Usually from 9:00 am to 11:00 pm. Double-check on holidays!
- **Entry Fee:** Varies, but investing in a Firenze Card might save you bucks across sites.
- **Nearby Bites:** The piazza outside is peppered with cafes. Espresso, anyone?

- **Trivia Tidbit:** Beneath the palace? Ancient Roman ruins. Because, of course, even Florence's basements are artsy.
- **Dress Code:** Respectful attire. Leave those beach flip-flops for...well, the beach.

Basilica of Santa Croce

Whoever said "rest in peace" never met the illustrious guests of the Basilica of Santa Croce. It's basically the VIP lounge for eternal resting - hosting celebs like Michelangelo, Galileo, and Rossini. Sure, they're not exactly up for a chat, but their legacies speak volumes.

Ever had that feeling of walking into a room and being the least accomplished? Yep, this basilica is that room. But beyond the who's who of gravestones, the Gothic architecture whispers tales of devotion, and the frescoes provide a color palette that even the fanciest design software can't replicate.

Swift Santa Croce Scoop:

- **Location:** Piazza Santa Croce. Look for a structure with a gravitational pull on tourists.
- **Highlight:** Michelangelo's tomb, but also peek at the Pazzi Chapel.
- **Hours:** Generally 9:30 am to 5:30 pm. But holidays might be hard to get.
- **Entry Fee:** A few euros. Exact change is always a kind gesture.
- **Gastronomic Tip:** Wander the nearby lanes for gelaterias. A sweet treat post-sightseeing? Yes, please!
- **Neat Fact:** The basilica's floor? A celestial map! Look down and star-gaze.

- **Attire Tip:** It's a holy space, so cover those shoulders and knees.

So, while the Basilica of Santa Croce might sound like a solemn spot, remember: it's also where stars (of humankind) align. Onward, to legendary tales and Gothic allure!

The Accademia Gallery

Did Michelangelo sneak magic into his chisel? At The Accademia Gallery, one starts to wonder. The star of the show, David, isn't just a sculpture; he's the epitome of Renaissance swagger. Standing there, all 17 feet of him, he's less "ancient statue" and more "guy who's too cool for art school."

But don't let David hog all your attention. The gallery is like a candy store for art lovers, packed with works that'll make your eyes dance. From paintings to other masterful sculptures, the Accademia offers a veritable feast for the senses.

Rapid Rundown for The Accademia:

- **Location:** Via Ricasoli. The crowd outside is your hint!
- **Not-to-Miss:** 'Prisoners/Slaves' – Michelangelo's unfinished masterpieces.
- **Hours:** Typically 8:15 am to 6:50 pm. But double-check on holidays.
- **Entry Fee:** It varies, but reserving a ticket online can save you the notorious queue time.
- **Art-Lover Tip:** Check for temporary exhibitions. They often showcase splendid collections.
- **Shhh Secret:** David's not the only version. Spot the replicas around Florence and play 'Spot the Real David'!
- **Comfort Alert:** Wear comfy shoes; the marble floors, though regal, aren't the kindest to feet.

Boboli Gardens

Remember the childhood tales where gardens held whispers of forgotten legends? Well, Boboli might just be the grown-up, Italian version of that fantasy. It's not just a garden; it's an open-air museum with each path taking you to a different era, each pond reflecting more than just the Tuscan sky.

Fancy a stroll where Medici dukes once pondered the affairs of state? Or prefer discovering hidden grottoes that seem straight out of a fairy tale? Boboli doesn't just let you walk; it lets you time-travel, all while you're surrounded by impeccably manicured greenery and historic sculptures.

Quick Guide to Boboli's Magic:

- **Location:** Piazza Pitti. It's so expansive you'd think Florence is hiding inside!
- **Not-to-Miss:** The Amphitheater, Neptune's Fountain, and the Buontalenti Grotto. A bit of magic, some splashing, and a dash of drama!
- **Hours:** Opens at 8:15 am but closing varies from 4:30 pm in winter to 6:30 pm in summer.
- **Entry Fee:** There's a charge, but it's a ticket to serenity (and history). Discounts are available for kids and seniors.
- **Garden Guru Tip:** Wear a hat and carry some water, especially in summer. Boboli's charm can make you forget the Tuscan sun!
- **Picnic Pointer:** Grab some local cheese, olives, and bread for a delightful garden picnic. Remember, clean up after!

Florence's Hidden Gems

Every traveler has a story about that one café, alley, or hidden courtyard they stumbled upon that etched Florence into their hearts forever. These are places away from the crowds, where time seems to slow, allowing you to truly savor the spirit of the city.

Via del Corno: The Whispering Lane of Florence

If Florence's streets were chapters in a book, Via del Corno would be that engrossing tale you found hidden between the more celebrated stories. It's not one for the grand stage, but its subtle charm and quieter rhythm can be even more captivating for the true explorer.

Why It's Worth the Detour:

- **Intimate Atmosphere:** Unlike the bustle of Florence's main streets, Via del Corno offers an intimate peek into daily Florentine life. Laundry hanging across balconies, the soft hum of local chatter, and the occasional bicycle ringing its bell create an atmosphere that feels like a step back in time.

- **History Underfoot:** The cobblestones here have been worn down by countless footsteps. Some say that if you listen closely, you can hear the echoes of the past — from children playing to merchants peddling their wares.

- **Charming Eateries:** This lane boasts some quaint trattorias that aren't just tourist traps. Pop into one of them, and you're likely to find yourself seated next to a local. Order what they're having; it's bound to be delicious!

Local Tips & Practicalities:

- **Footwear:** Those charming cobblestones can be slightly treacherous, especially after rain. Ditch the heels and opt for comfortable walking shoes.

- **Snacking:** Seek out the local panini shop on the lane. Their fillings are a delightful mix of traditional ingredients with a modern twist. Plus, nothing beats a fresh panino when exploring.

- **Art Galore:** Keep an eye out for little art studios and galleries tucked away. You might just find a piece of art that resonates, created by a local artisan.

- **Nighttime Charm:** As dusk settles, Via del Corno takes on an ethereal charm. Lit by the warm glow of streetlights, it's the perfect setting for a romantic evening stroll.

La Specola

Look, I get it. When you think Florence, "natural history" isn't the first thing that pops into your mind. But let's shake things up a bit. Welcome to La Specola, Florence's oldest public museum. And oh boy, it's not your typical, dusty exhibit space.

Why It's Worth the Detour:

- **A Room Full of Surprises:** Remember those old cabinets of curiosities? La Specola is like stepping into one but super-sized. From fossils to stuffed exotic animals, it's a veritable Aladdin's cave for the curious.

- **Wax Anatomical Models:** Not for the faint-hearted, but utterly fascinating. La Specola houses one of the world's largest collections of wax anatomical models from the 18th century. It's a peek into the human body like you've never seen before.

- **Stellar Views:** Pardon the pun, but 'specola' translates to 'observatory.' Climb to the top, and you'll be rewarded with panoramic views of Florence. It's a whole new way to see the city, with the Duomo gracing the horizon.

Local Tips & Practicalities:

- **Visit Timing:** Try to visit during weekday mornings. It tends to be less crowded, allowing you to truly delve into the exhibits without elbowing your way through.

- **Sensitive Content:** A heads-up! Some of the anatomical exhibits can be graphic. If you're with kids or someone squeamish, you might want to skip that section.

- **Photography:** While you can snap photos in most parts of the museum, some areas might have restrictions. Always check for signage or ask a staff member.

- **Budget Time:** Set aside at least 2 hours for your visit. There's a lot to explore, and you don't want to rush through the museum's 34 rooms.

- **Gift Shop Alert:** Before you exit, make a pit stop at the gift shop. It's packed with quirky souvenirs that are a far cry from your standard postcards and keychains.

Brancacci Chapel

Ever had a painting leave you a little breathless, a smidge teary-eyed, or just full-on awestruck? If not, brace yourself, because Brancacci Chapel is about to change that for you. Nestled unassumingly within the Church of Santa Maria del Carmine, this gem might look modest from the outside, but its walls are bursting with tales of genius and rivalry.

Why It's Worth the Detour:

- **A Fresco Feast:** Masaccio's frescoes here are hailed as the Renaissance's coming-of-age story. His 'Expulsion from the Garden of Eden' isn't just paint on a wall; it's raw emotion and a masterclass in perspective and light.

- **Historic Rivalries:** Fun fact: Masolino started the frescoes, Masaccio took over, and Filippino Lippi finished it. Imagine being the art mediator in that room. Drama aside, it's fascinating to see the evolution of styles side-by-side.

- **Artistic Epiphanies:** Artists like Michelangelo were known to visit, study, and draw inspiration from these frescoes. So, you're quite literally tracing the footsteps of the greats.

Local Tips & Practicalities:

- **Booking Ahead:** The chapel regulates the number of visitors to prevent damage to the frescoes. So, snag a reservation to guarantee your spot.

- **Guided Tour:** Splurge on a guided tour if you can. The stories behind each fresco add layers to what you're seeing.

- **Wear Respectful Attire:** Remember, it's a place of worship. Stick to attire that covers shoulders and knees.

- **Limit Flash:** If you're hoping to capture the beauty, remember flash photography is a no-go. Honestly, though, photos don't do justice. Sometimes, it's best to just soak it all in.

- **Duration:** Give yourself a good hour here. Each fresco has a story, and you'll want the time to appreciate every brushstroke.

Pharmacy of Santa Maria Novella

Ever walked into a place and thought, "Did I accidentally invent time travel?" Welcome to the Pharmacy of Santa Maria Novella, one of the world's oldest pharmacies, but don't expect fluorescent lights and generic pill bottles. This is where alchemical magic meets luxury.

Why It's Worth the Detour:

- **Sensory Overload:** Every shelf here is laden with exquisite perfumes, artisanal soaps, and potpourris that have been made using age-old recipes. Inhale deeply and feel centuries of craftsmanship in every scent.

- **A History Buff's Dream:** Founded by Dominican friars in the 13th century, this place once created remedies during the time of the plague. Talk about resilience!

- **Architectural Eye-Candy:** Ornate wooden shelves, frescoed ceilings, and stained-glass windows make you feel like you're in an art museum, not a store.

Local Tips & Practicalities:

- **Take the Tour:** It's not just about buying things. They offer guided tours where you learn about the history and process of creating their legendary products.

- **Sample Galore:** The staff are generous with samples. If something catches your nose, ask to try!

- **Bring Some Euros:** While they do accept cards, sometimes old-world charm pairs best with some good old cash.

- **Unique Souvenirs:** Looking for gifts that scream 'thoughtful'? Their Rosewater or the Calendula cream are both hits.

Stibbert Museum

Fancy an eclectic mix of knights' armor, Egyptian mummies, and Renaissance art? Sounds a bit like someone threw darts at a list of "cool historical stuff," right? Well, that someone was Frederick Stibbert, and his eccentric collection is our gain.

Why It's Worth the Detour:

- **Knight in Shining Armor:** The museum boasts one of the most extensive collections of European, Islamic, and Japanese armory. If you've ever wondered how knights geared up for a fight, this is your place.

- **Worldly Wonders:** Stibbert was a globe-trotter, and his diverse collection spans continents. From Egyptian artifacts to Japanese samurai swords, it's a worldly journey without the jet lag.

- **A Homey Affair:** Unlike traditional museums, this was Stibbert's home. You're essentially wandering through a history enthusiast's personal mansion. How's that for intimacy?

Local Tips & Practicalities:

- **Guided Tours Only:** You can only see the museum with a guide. It's a good thing, trust us. The stories are half the fun!

- **Garden Galore:** Don't miss the gardens! They're a peaceful oasis and a perfect spot for those "I'm deep in thought" photos.

- **Convenient Location:** Located just outside the main city, it's a short cab or bus ride away.

- **Time it Right:** The museum sometimes holds nighttime events with the armory lit up. It's eerie, atmospheric, and mesmerizing.

Delving Deeper: Florentine Specialties and Experiences

If you're seeking an authentic taste of Florence beyond the postcard spots, get ready! Here are some regional treasures and experiences, straight from a local's playbook:

Sip on a Negroni: While everyone's gushing about Italian wines (and rightly so), take a moment to appreciate Florence's gift to the cocktail world. Born in Florence, the Negroni - a mix of gin, vermouth rosso, and Campari - is a must-try. Find a quaint bar, ask for a "Negroni, per favore," and watch the world go by.

Savor Florentine Steak: Called 'Bistecca alla Fiorentina', this T-bone steak is seasoned with just salt, grilled to perfection, and typically served rarely. It's simple, hearty, and the very essence of Tuscan cuisine.

Dive into Artisan Workshops: Florence isn't just about the art in museums. Venture into Oltrarno, where you'll discover tiny workshops of artisans sculpting, crafting leather, and more. They're the unsung heroes keeping the city's craft legacy alive.

Treasure Hunt at San Lorenzo Market: Forget souvenirs. Head to this bustling market for leather goods, vintage finds, and those special trinkets you won't get elsewhere.

Lampredotto Sandwich, Anyone? It's a Florentine street food classic. Made from the fourth stomach of a cow, it might sound outlandish, but trust the locals: it's deliciously tender and uniquely Florentine.

Sunset at Piazzale Michelangelo: Sure, every guidebook mentions this. But a local tip? Bring some local cheese, cured meats, and a bottle of Chianti. Transform it into a memorable picnic with an iconic view.

Florentine Paper Magic: Step into one of the city's paper shops, where marbled paper is crafted with a design technique dating back to the 12th century. Pick a journal or some stationery, and you've got yourself a piece of art.

Key Takeaways

- **Unrivaled Artistic Legacy:** Florence, as the cradle of the Renaissance, houses some of the world's most iconic art and architectural wonders. Venues like the Uffizi Gallery and Accademia Gallery are more than just museums; they're time capsules of creative brilliance.

- **Blend of Famous & Hidden Gems:** While the Florence Cathedral and Ponte Vecchio are on every tourist's list, the city has countless lesser-known attractions that offer equally enriching experiences.

- **Authentic Florentine Flavors:** From sipping a local Negroni to relishing a Lampredotto sandwich, Florence offers a gastronomic journey that is both traditional and unique.

- **Local Insights are Gold:** Engaging with local artisans, shopping in traditional markets, and embracing regional specialties provide a genuine understanding of Florence's rich cultural tapestry.

Action Steps

- **Plan Ahead, but Leave Room for Spontaneity:** While you must book tickets for popular attractions in advance (like the Uffizi), ensure you have unscheduled time to explore off-the-beaten-path spots.

- **Engage with Locals:** Strike up a conversation with the cafe owner or the artisan in his workshop. Their insights and stories can lead you to experiences not found in guidebooks.

- **Prioritize According to Passion:** Are you a foodie? Dive into the local markets and eateries. An art lover? Prioritize galleries and artisan workshops. Customize your Florence journey according to what excites you the most.

- **Pack Comfortably:** Florence is best explored on foot. Comfortable shoes and a day pack for essentials like water, snacks, and a map can make your wandering more pleasant.

- **Document Your Journey:** Whether it's through photographs, journal entries, or even sketches, document your unique Florentine experiences. Not only will it serve as a cherished memory, but it can also be your personal guide for friends and family.

Remember, Florence isn't just a city to be visited; it's an experience to be lived. Dive deep, keep an open heart, and let the city's magic unfold at every step.

Chapter 3: A Taste of Florence - Culinary Delights

"Florence – the city of tranquility made manifest."

– Katherine Cecil Thurston

You know, if food were a language, Florence would be poetry. Beyond the gilded domes and cobblestone alleys, this city sings a symphony of flavors that have captivated palates for centuries. It's not just about indulging in a meal; it's a dance of traditions, stories, and passion plated up for you. Ready to whet your appetite? In this chapter, we're delving deep into Florence's gastronomic wonders, from the iconic dishes that have stood the test of time to the contemporary twists on old classics. Fork and knife in hand, let's feast our way through the culinary heart of Tuscany.

Florence's Unique Culinary History and Its Evolution

Medieval Munchies: During the Middle Ages, Florentines weren't dining on truffle-laden pasta. Nope, they kept it simple with spelt soups and saltless bread. Ever wondered why traditional Florentine bread lacks salt? Legend says it's due to a tax war with Pisa, but locals might just tell you it's to better accompany the region's bold flavors.

Renaissance Rhapsody: Enter the era of opulence! The Renaissance period wasn't just about arts and science; it was also about lavish feasts. Think of big tables decked with roast meats, elaborate sugar sculptures, and the introduction of forks. Yup, Florence said goodbye to messy fingers before much of Europe!

19th Century Flair: Here's when things got a tad more familiar. This era saw the birth of gelato (thank you, Florence!) and a move towards lighter, more herb-infused dishes. The city's culinary scene started to reflect its cosmopolitan character.

Modern Mouthfuls: Fast forward to today, and Florence is a melting pot of its storied past and global influences. You'll find traditional Tuscan trattorias right next to hipster cafes brewing up artisanal coffees. The classics, like ribollita and pappa al pomodoro, still hold their ground, but with a sprinkle of contemporary zest.

A Florentine Foodie's Bucket List

- **Bistecca alla Fiorentina:**

  What it is: A thick, juicy T-bone steak, usually grilled to perfection and seasoned with just olive oil, rosemary, and a sprinkle of salt.
  Local's Tip: Head to Trattoria Mario near the central market. It's bustling, with long communal tables, and you might have to wait for a seat, but oh boy, is it worth it. Remember, this steak is usually ordered by weight, so bring a friend or a massive appetite!

- **Ribollita:**

  What it is: A hearty soup made of bread, beans, and veggies. It's rustic, filling, and the epitome of Tuscan comfort food.
  Local's Tip: For a bowl that tastes like nonna (grandma) made it, try La Casalinga. It's an old-school eatery, tucked away from the main streets, frequented by locals.

- **Lampredotto:**

  What it is: Not for the faint-hearted, it's a sandwich filled with the fourth stomach of a cow, typically seasoned and served with green sauce or spicy oil.
  Local's Tip: Head to Da Nerbone in the Central Market. It's a stand-up stall, but their lampredotto sandwich has a cult following.

- **Gelato:**

  What it is: Italian ice cream, but oh-so-creamy and delectable.
  Local's Tip: Skip the touristy spots and head straight to Gelateria La Carraia. Their flavors are rich, and locals swear by the authenticity.

- **Pappa al Pomodoro:**

  What it is: A thick tomato and bread soup, drizzled with good quality olive oil.
  Local's Tip: Il Santo Bevitore offers a modern twist to this classic, served amidst a chic ambiance without losing the dish's rustic charm.

- **Cantucci & Vin Santo:**

  What it is: Almond biscuits you dip into a sweet wine. A delightful end to any Tuscan meal.
  Local's Tip: For a truly traditional experience, visit Cantinetta Antinori. Housed in a Renaissance palace, you can savor the biscuits and wine combo, feeling like Florentine royalty.

- **Schiaicciata All'Olio:**

What it is: A soft, olive oil-rich flatbread sprinkled with salt. It's slightly crispy on the outside and delightfully fluffy inside.

Local's Tip: Forno Pugi is an institution when it comes to this treat. Grab one fresh out of the oven and savor it as you stroll through the city.

- **Torta Della Nonna:**

What it is: Literally translates to "Grandmother's cake." It's a delicious pastry filled with creamy custard and topped with pine nuts.

Local's Tip: Visit Caffè Gilli in Piazza della Repubblica. Established in 1733, their Torta Della Nonna is nothing short of perfection.

- **Crocchè di Patate:**

What it is: Mashed potato croquettes, lightly crispy on the outside and melt-in-your-mouth soft inside.

Local's Tip: Street vendors and local "rosticcerias" (roast meat shops) typically have the best ones. Be on the lookout for queues of locals – that's where the magic happens.

- **Trippa alla Fiorentina:**

What it is: Tripe stewed in a rich tomato sauce. It might sound challenging, but its flavor will win you over!

Local's Tip: Head over to Sergio Gozzi. It's a simple trattoria that has been serving this delicacy for over a century.

- **Panzanella:**

What it is: A refreshing bread salad with tomatoes, onions, cucumbers, and fresh basil, all soaked in olive oil and vinegar.

Local's Tip: Trattoria Sostanza serves up a hearty portion that feels like summer in a bowl.

- **Affogato:**
  What it is: A scoop of vanilla gelato "drowned" in a shot of hot espresso. Simplicity at its best.
  Local's Tip: At Caffè Rivoire, you get an Affogato with a view, as it overlooks the bustling Piazza della Signoria.

Lesser known But Incredibly Tasty Florentine Foods and Drinks

Florence's culinary scene isn't just about its famous dishes; it also boasts a range of lesser-known delights that are true hidden gems. Here's your guide to the undercover stars of Florentine cuisine:

- **Pappa al Pomodoro:**

What it is: A thick, hearty bread soup made with ripe tomatoes, garlic, basil, and olive oil. While known to some, it remains a hidden treasure to many travelers.

Local's Tip: Osteria dell'Enoteca offers an authentic rendition of this dish that truly encapsulates Tuscan comfort food.

- **Peposo:**

What it is: A rich, peppery beef stew that dates back to the Renaissance era. Its slow-cooked tenderness is a testament to patience yielding delicious results.

Local's Tip: Trattoria Mario near the Central Market is your go-to. It's a lunchtime-only spot, so plan accordingly!

- **Lampredotto Sandwich:**

What it is: Made from the fourth stomach of the cow, it's Florence's street food star. Simmered till tender and served in a crusty roll with salsa verde, this delicacy is both bold and delicious.

Local's Tip: For the bravest foodies, street carts around the city serve this. Look for carts with queues of locals, like Lampredotto da Nerbone in the Central Market.

- **Fagioli all'uccelletto:**

What it is: A savory concoction of beans baked in tomato sauce with sage and garlic. It's Tuscan comfort in a bowl.

Local's Tip: Head to Trattoria da Rocco, a family-run spot known for their warm ambiance and genuine Florentine flavors.

- **Vin Santo e Cantuccini:**

What it is: This is a duo of almond biscotti dipped in a sweet dessert wine. Perfect to conclude a hearty Florentine meal.

Local's Tip: While many places serve this classic pairing, Enoteca Pinchiorri offers an experience par excellence with its extensive wine collection.

- **Acqua Cotta:**

What it is: Translating to "cooked water," this is a traditional Tuscan soup made from stale bread, vegetables, and broth. Simplicity at its most flavorful.

Local's Tip: Osteria del Cinghiale Bianco not only serves a fantastic Acqua Cotta but also offers a cozy ambiance reminiscent of old Flonce.

Key Takeaways

- **Historical Culinary Insight:**
  - Florence has a rich gastronomic history influenced by political, economic, and artistic movements.
  - The Renaissance period brought a culinary evolution, emphasizing fresh, local ingredients.

- **Flagship Dishes:**
  - Bistecca alla Fiorentina: T-bone steak, grilled to perfection.
  - Ribollita: Hearty bread and vegetable soup, a Tuscan staple.
  - Tagliatelle Funghi Porcini e Tartufo: Pasta with mushrooms and truffles.

- **Hidden Gastronomic Gems:**
  - Pappa al Pomodoro: Tomato-bread soup, the epitome of Tuscan comfort.
  - Peposo: Peppery beef stew with historical roots.
  - Lampredotto Sandwich: A bold street food star made from the cow's fourth stomach.
  - Fagioli all'uccelletto: Beans baked in a savory tomato sauce.
  - Vin Santo e Cantuccini: Almond biscotti paired with sweet dessert wine.

- **Drinks to Try:**
  - Chianti: Renowned red wine from the Tuscan region.
  - Negroni: Famous Florentine cocktail with gin, vermouth, and Campari.

- **Dining Tips:**

- Explore local markets for fresh ingredients and authentic food stalls.
- Dine where the locals do to discover the true essence of Florentine cuisine.
- Consider time-of-day specialties, like the afternoon aperitivo.

Action Steps

- **Market Morning:** Start your day early with a visit to Mercato Centrale. Engage with local vendors, sample fresh produce, and maybe even buy ingredients for a DIY Tuscan meal.

- **Steak Challenge:** Dare yourself to finish an entire Bistecca alla Fiorentina at a traditional osteria. Remember, it's best enjoyed medium-rare!

- **Cooking Class:** Book a local cooking class. Learn to prepare classic Florentine dishes from scratch and take the recipes home as delicious souvenirs.

- **Wine Tasting:** Venture to a wine shop or enoteca and ask for a Chianti tasting. Learn to swirl, sniff, and sip like a true connoisseur.

- **Local Recommendations:** Engage with locals and ask for their favorite dining spots. Often, the best places aren't in guidebooks but in the hearts of the people who live there.

- **Document Your Culinary Journey:** Keep a food journal or start a social media page dedicated to your Tuscan culinary adventures. It's a fun way to reminisce later and share recommendations with friends.

Chapter 4: Live Like a Local

"I've always considered Florence as my girlfriend. I don't have to explain my love for this city."

- Gabriel Batistuta

You know, there's a secret Florentine club. No, it's not behind some velvet rope, guarded by a burly bouncer. It's out there on the cobblestone streets, in the bustling piazzas, and down the quaint alleyways. Every local is a member, and here's the best part: they're offering you an honorary membership! All you need to do? Toss out that tourist map, slip into your most comfortable shoes, and dive headfirst into the rhythm of Florentine life. Welcome to "Living Like a Local 101." Class is now in session!

San Frediano

San Frediano is where vintage meets vogue. Nestled in the Oltrarno district, this neighborhood is like that artsy cousin who studied abroad and came back with cool stories and an edgy haircut. Artisan workshops dot the streets, local boutiques showcase the coolest threads, and the walls? They tell tales in murals and graffiti. It's not just Lonely Planet that's fanboying over this place; so will you. The cherry on top? Gelato from La Sorbettiera that'll make you rethink all your life's ice cream choices.

- **Location:** Situated in the Oltrarno district.
- **What's Special:** This neighborhood boasts a bohemian vibe, filled with artisan workshops and local boutiques.
- **Local Tip:** Don't miss out on "Borgo San Frediano," recently declared one of the coolest neighborhoods in the

world by Lonely Planet. Make sure to grab a gelato at La Sorbettiera and marvel at the local street art.

Le Cure

Le Cure is like Florence's best-kept secret, whispered only among locals. North of the historic center, this neighborhood is away from the usual hustle. Here, every day feels like a Sunday morning. There's a relaxed air, with folks exchanging stories at the local market, kids playing in the parks, and the scent of home-cooked meals wafting through. Want to channel your inner chef? Those fresh tomatoes from the market are waiting to be turned into a tangy pasta sauce.

- **Location:** North of the historic center.
- **What's Special:** A residential area with a bustling local market and tranquil parks, perfect for people watching.
- **Local Tip:** The daily market here is a treasure trove for fresh produce. Perfect for those wanting to attempt cooking a Florentine dish in their Airbnb!

Campo di Marte

Think of Campo di Marte as that sporty friend who's always up for a game and rarely runs out of energy. Located east of the city center, it's the beating heart for sports enthusiasts. The roar of the crowd from the stadium, the passionate debates about the latest football match at local cafes, it's all here. And if you happen to wear purple, the unofficial color of camaraderie here, you might just get a cheerful nod from the locals.

- **Location:** East of the city center.
- **What's Special:** Sports enthusiasts, this is your haven! It houses the main stadium of Florence.

- **Local Tip:** Catch a Fiorentina football match if you can. But remember, wear something purple - that's the team color!

San Niccolò

San Niccolò has the air of an old poet - wise, serene, and with a touch of bohemian. Located at the base of the Piazzale Michelangelo, this area is like Florence's thoughtful nook. The streets are quieter, but there's a hum of creativity, with young artists sketching by the corners, antique shops showcasing history, and cafes playing soft melodies. And if you're a fan of sunsets? The Rose Garden isn't just any garden; it's THE place for those golden hour views.

- **Location:** Base of the Piazzale Michelangelo.
- **What's Special:** Brimming with Renaissance history, it's quieter with a lot of young artists flocking here.
- **Local Tip:** For those seeking serenity with a view, grab a bottle of Chianti and head to the Rose Garden (Giardino delle Rose) during sunset.

Coverciano

Coverciano is the ultimate crossroad of football and history. Imagine a neighborhood where every second person is either discussing last night's match or planning the next one. And amidst these discussions, the historic charm of Florence isn't lost. The Italian Football Federation's Technical Center stands as a testament to the country's love for the sport. Even if football isn't your calling, the museum here might just make you a fan. Or at least, teach you enough to blend in with the local chatter.

- **Location:** Southeast of the historic center.
- **What's Special:** It's where football meets history, hosting the Italian Football Federation's Technical Center.

- **Local Tip:** Soccer aficionados, the Football Museum here is your pitstop. Brush up on your Italian football trivia before you go.

Local Customs and Traditions

Tip or Not to Tip?

While tipping isn't mandatory in Florence like it is in the US, a little extra for good service (especially in restaurants) is always appreciated. But don't break the bank—just round up the bill or leave some change.

Keep the Volume Down

Florentines aren't the loudest bunch. Keep conversations, especially in public places, at a moderate volume. They'll appreciate you not turning public buses into personal phone booths.

Fashion Matters

Florence is the fashion capital's older, classy sibling. While you don't need to strut around in runway-worthy ensembles, a neat and polished look is admired. Save the beachwear for the beach!

Punctuality is a Virtue…Kinda

Be on time if you're invited to someone's home. But for casual outings, being a teeny bit late is often forgiven (or expected). But don't push it too far!

Embrace the Passeggiata

Evening strolls, or "passeggiata", are a cherished Italian tradition. Join in! Stroll around, enjoy the city's beauty, and maybe grab a gelato. Yes, every evening is an ice-cream evening here.

Kiss-Kiss, Hello!

Don't be startled if you're greeted with a kiss on both cheeks. It's a common form of greeting among friends. Remember, it's the right cheek first. Or was it left? Eh, just go with the flow.

Table Manners

Hands on the table (not elbows), and please, oh please, don't ask for ketchup with your pasta. You might get some side-eye glances.

Closed for Siesta

Many smaller shops and restaurants might close in the afternoon for a short break. It's not them; it's the tradition. Plan your shopping sprees accordingly.

Beware of the "Coperto"

Many restaurants charge a small fee called "coperto" which is a cover charge. It's standard, so don't be surprised when it appears on your bill.

Church Etiquette

When entering churches, modesty is key. Women should cover their shoulders, and both men and women are expected to wear clothes that at least cover the knees.

Tips On How to Truly Immerse Yourself in Florentine Culture

1. **Coffee Like a Local**
   Forget your venti caramel macchiato! Go for a quick shot of espresso at the bar, stand tall, sip it down, and be on your way. It's the Florentine caffeine kick.

2. **Master the Art of Haggling**
   Those market stalls aren't just for admiring. Flex those negotiation muscles at San Lorenzo Market. Just remember: charm first, then a little playfulness. And if the price doesn't budge? It's all part of the game.

3. **Attend a Cooking Class**
   Whip up a storm with Tuscan recipes. Let's face it, wouldn't it be cool to say you can make authentic Ribollita or Pappa al Pomodoro?

4. **Get Lost (Purposefully)**
   Ditch Google Maps for an afternoon. Wander aimlessly. You might discover a hidden gem of a trattoria or a serene spot away from the tourist hustle.

5. **Florentine Festivals**
   Keep an eye out for local festivals. "La Rificolona" in September is a lantern festival that feels straight out of a fairy tale.

6. **Two Words: Wine Tasting**
   You're in Tuscany, for goodness sake. Learn what makes a Chianti classic or why Brunello di Montalcino is adored globally. Sip, swirl, repeat.

7. **Park Hangs**

Mingle with locals at the city's green spots. Bring some cheese, a bottle of wine, and make an impromptu picnic. You might even pick up some local gossip.

8. **Local Cinema**
Florentines love their films. Check out an open-air movie in the summer months. Even if it's in Italian, the atmosphere is universally delightful.

9. **Speak a Lil' Italian**
While "Ciao" and "Grazie" are a good start, locals love it when you sprinkle in a bit more. "Che bello!" (How beautiful!) is an easy and always-applicable phrase.

10. **Attend A Soccer Match**

Feel the city's pulse by joining the roaring crowds at a Fiorentina soccer game. Even if you don't know the rules, just cheer when they do.

Key Takeaways

- **Neighborhood Nuances:** Florence is more than its city center. Dive deep into neighborhoods like Oltrarno, Le Cure, and Campo di Marte to find authentic local vibes.

- **Coffee Culture:** Sip espresso the local way—quickly at the bar and sans frills.

- **Negotiation 101:** At markets like San Lorenzo, a touch of charm and playfulness can score you a good deal.

- **Culinary Craft:** Taking a cooking class not only enriches your palette but also connects you to Tuscan traditions.

- **Map-less Marvel:** Sometimes, the best treasures in Florence are found when you let your feet guide you rather than a GPS.

- **Festival Fun:** Engage in local festivities, like "La Rificolona," to truly feel the city's spirit.

- **Vino Ventures:** Embrace Tuscany's wine legacy through tastings and understanding the stories behind each pour.

- **Park Picnics:** City parks are your gateway to laid-back Florentine living; grab some cheese and wine, and you're set!

- **Cinematic Charm:** Open-air movies during summer are a delight, showcasing the Florentine love for films.

- **Lingo Love:** Picking up more Italian phrases will only endear you more to locals.

- **Sports Spirit:** Feeling the rush at a Fiorentina soccer game encapsulates the passionate pulse of the city.

Action Steps

- **Stroll and Survey:** Set a morning to wander Oltrarno or Campo di Marte without a plan. Follow the aromas, the music, or even a local's recommendation.

- **Espresso Experiment:** Visit a local coffee bar tomorrow morning. Stand, sip, and observe the rhythm of local life.

- **Market Mission:** Dedicate a morning to San Lorenzo market. Try negotiating a price or simply engage the vendors in a chat about their wares.

- **Cooking Commitment:** Book a traditional Tuscan cooking class this week. Learn, cook, eat, repeat!

- **Picnic Prep:** Buy local cheeses, cured meats, and a bottle of Chianti. Head to a city park for an afternoon picnic.

- **Festival Find:** Check the local calendar for any upcoming festivals or events. Make it a point to attend at least one during your stay.

- **Vino Voyage:** Visit a local enoteca (wine shop) and ask for recommendations on Tuscan wines. Enjoy a glass in the evening.

- **Movie Magic:** Find an open-air movie schedule. Watch at least one classic Italian film under the Florentine night sky.

- **Language Leap:** Each day, learn and use five new Italian phrases. Ask locals for pronunciation help!

- **Sports Step:** If the season's right, buy a ticket to a Fiorentina soccer game. Wear purple and cheer with the crowd.

- **Gift Grab:** Buy something artisanal from a local craftsman—a memento of your immersive Florentine journey.

Conclusion

Florence, with its harmonious blend of the past and the present, has sung its mesmerizing siren song, and, by now, you must be utterly entranced. It's hard not to be, right?

From the cobblestone streets that still echo the footfalls of art and science giants in Chapter 1, to the awe-inspiring structures and hidden gems that pepper the cityscape in Chapter 2, every corner of Florence breathes a legacy. You've learned to appreciate this beautiful city not just as a tourist but as a true art and history enthusiast.

And who could forget the gustatory pleasures we dipped into in Chapter 3? Ah, the tantalizing flavors of Florentine cuisine! The lavish dishes and those hidden culinary secrets tucked away in nondescript lanes are sure to make your taste buds reminisce long after you've departed.

Then, in Chapter 4, we brushed away the veneer of 'tourist' and painted you with the hues of a local, unveiling Florence in its most genuine and vibrant shades.

Now, as all good things inch towards a pause, here's a last sprinkle of wisdom: Let Florence be more than just a checkmark on your travel list. Every time you sip an espresso or spot a piece of Renaissance art elsewhere, let it be a time machine transporting you back to the golden streets of this city. And hey, always remember to wear comfortable shoes, keep that local phrasebook handy, and be ready for impromptu gelato stops!

Lastly, as you close this book with dreams of Florence still dancing in your eyes, know that Italy has more gems in its trove. Glistening waters, romantic gondolas, and masked balls beckon. Venice awaits you in the next leg of our Italy Travel Guide series. Until then, keep your wanderlust alive, and as the Italians say, "Viaggi sicuri!" - Travel safely!

Book 3

Venice Travel Guide

Explore to Win

Introduction

"In memory Venice is always magic."

– Barbara Grizzuti Harrison

Ever felt like the world has gotten too small, too...predictable? You scroll through travel blogs, Instagram stories, or those '10 Places to Visit Before You Die' lists, and everything starts to look the same. What if I told you there's a place that defies all travel stereotypes? No, it's not another secret tropical island or an undiscovered hiking trail. It's Venice—the city that doesn't believe in roads, where GPS confuses tourists and locals alike, and where your morning commute might just be via a gondola.

Now, I know what you're thinking: "Venice? Isn't that just for honeymooners or people who want to reenact scenes from 'The Tourist'?" Trust me; it's easy to get entangled in the touristy web spun around iconic destinations like Venice. That's why this guide is hell-bent on setting things straight, for once and for all.

Here's your dilemma: You're tantalized by the images of Venice, but you don't want to end up holding a plastic carnival mask, trapped in an overpriced gondola, and missing out on the city's authentic charm. Fair point! And that's exactly what we're going to tackle in this guide. You'll get tips so local, you'll question whether they were meant to be shared with outsiders at all. We're talking secret café corners, hushed art galleries, and experiences that will make your friends back home drop their pumpkin spice lattes in envy.

As for who's feeding you this insider knowledge—let's just say my feet have kissed more cobblestones, and my taste buds have explored more back-alley eateries than I care to count. Years of gallivanting around Venice and mingling with locals have culminated in this guide.

By now, you're probably wondering why you should trust this guide over the countless others vying for your attention. Well, it's simple: authenticity. The goal of this guide is not to rush you through the most Instagrammable spots for quick likes and follows. This is about showing you Venice in its most sincere form—the Venice that Venetians love and experience daily. We'll dive into traditions so deeply rooted that even the ebb and flow of the tides bow in respect. You'll find yourself navigating narrow canals and hidden alleys like a seasoned local, avoiding the overcrowded tourist traps like the plague.

Oh, and let's not forget the food! No more Googling "best pasta near me" and ending up in some subpar tourist hangout. We're going to places where the locals go, eateries where recipes have been passed down from generation to generation. Trust me, your taste buds will thank you.

You see, the Venice you're about to discover is more than just a city; it's a feeling, an experience, and a story waiting to be told. As your unofficial Venice aficionado, it's my mission to ensure that your trip is as magical as the city itself.

Now that we've got all of that out of the way, what are you waiting for? This isn't just another guide; this is your golden ticket to experiencing Venice the way it was meant to be. You can forget about all the typical touristy nonsense. We're about to go on an adventure that you'll be sharing stories about for years to come.

Stay with me, and you won't just 'see' Venice; you'll live it. Turn the page, let's make some memories that no camera can capture and no postcard can convey.

Welcome to Venice—let's make it unforgettable!

Chapter 1: Venice Unmasked - The City Beyond the Canals

"An orange gem resting on a blue glass plate: it's Venice seen from above."

– Henry James

So, you think you know Venice? Gondolas, canals, and Carnival masks—oh my! But hold on a minute. Before you pack your bags and start practicing your "Ciao, bella!", let's dig deeper. Sure, Venice offers those iconic experiences, but it's also a place where each narrow alley whispers secrets and every sun-drenched plaza is a canvas of local life. Forget what you think you know about this floating marvel; we're diving headfirst into the authentic Venice that the postcards miss. Ready? Andiamo!

Why Venice is Unique

Floating Masterpiece: Unlike any other city in the world, Venice is an archipelago of 118 islands, interconnected by hundreds of bridges and scenic canals. It's a labyrinth you'll want to get lost in, where every turn yields a new, breathtaking vista.

Architectural Melting Pot: Gothic facades sit comfortably next to Byzantine mosaics and Renaissance palaces. The city is a living museum, but one where the buildings talk—if only you listen.

Masked and Marvelous: You may know about the famous Carnival, but did you know that masks are deeply ingrained in Venetian culture year-round? It's not just about hiding; it's about becoming someone—or something—utterly different for a while.

The Silent Serenade: Imagine a city where the constant hum of cars is replaced by the lapping of water against ancient stone walls and the harmonious choruses of boatmen. That's Venice for you.

Local Eats & Treats: Forget pizza and pasta for a moment—Venice has its unique culinary signature. From fresh seafood to cicchetti (local tapas), your taste buds are in for a treat.

The Engineering Marvel and the Sinking Dilemma

Venice is a city rising from the water, standing tall on wooden stilts pounded deep into the marshy ground. The place is an engineering conundrum, a defy-all-odds construction that proves human ingenuity knows no bounds. But here's the kicker—this marvel is sinking, and not so slowly anymore.

Venetians back in the day, around the 5th century, drove wooden pilings into the swampy lagoon bed. On top of those pilings, they laid marble platforms. The wood is petrified now, made rock-hard from centuries underwater without air. Venice isn't just built on islands; it's built on the water, an architectural feat that's both awe-inspiring and eyebrow-raising.

But what about the sinking? Well, Venice descends about 1 to 2 millimeters each year. Doesn't sound like a lot, right? But add that up over decades, and we've got a city with its feet—er, stilts—in water, quite literally. Climate change and rising sea levels accelerate this sinking feeling, giving a whole new urgency to the phrase "going under."

So, what's the city doing about it? Ever heard of MOSE? It's a series of barriers designed to block those pesky high tides from flooding the city. It's one of the many lifelines thrown to save Venice from becoming an underwater relic.

The sinking city is more than a tale of architectural audacity; it's a dramatic, real-world cliffhanger with Venice in the starring role. So when you're walking those ancient cobblestone streets or gliding through canals, just remember—you're literally above centuries of history, teetering on stilts, in a city that's fighting to stick around for the next act. How's that for a slice of Venetian drama?

Navigating the Venetian Lagoon: The Vaporetto Way

The Unsung Hero: No, it's not a Marvel character; the Vaporetto is Venice's water bus, and it's about as heroic as public transport can get. It crisscrosses canals, shuttling both locals and visitors from point A to point B. Forget taxis; the Vaporetto gives you the best views of Venice for a fraction of the cost.

Unbeatable Sunset Spot: Take the Vaporetto Line 1 in the evening, and you'll get sunset views that even Instagram can't do justice to. Golden hour in Venice isn't just a time; it's an experience.

Multi-Ticket Magic: You can get a tourist travel card offering unlimited use of the city's public transport network. It's a wallet-saver, especially if you're here for a few days.

Not Just for Tourists: Yes, the Vaporetto is a savior for tourists, but watch the locals—they know the secret shortcuts. Don't just stick to the Grand Canal; explore smaller routes for a slice of authentic Venice.

Seat or No Seat: If you're only going a couple of stops, feel free to stand. But for a longer, more scenic route like the Grand Canal, grab a seat. Your feet will thank you.

Know Your Stops: Don't expect loud announcements or neon signs. Keep an eye out and make use of the route map to avoid missing your stop.

Night Owl Advantage: Some Vaporetto lines run 24/7. So, if you've spent the night bar-hopping or simply soaking up the moonlit magic, you're covered.

The Venice Time Machine

The Merchant Maestro: Venice wasn't just any port city; it was the grandmaster of trade in medieval Europe. Ever heard of the Silk Road? Venice was the luxurious endpoint where East finally met West. Picture it: Exotic spices, fine silks, and even color-changing stones that fueled myths and legends.

Artistic Revolution: Think the Renaissance was all about Florence? Think again. Venice had its own circle of genius artists like Titian and Tintoretto, who flipped the script on classical art and made the world rethink beauty. Do you know those mind-blowing Venetian masks? Imagine an entire era masked in awe.

Tourist Mecca Before It Was Cool: Venice wasn't just a hotspot for traders and artists; it was the original vacation getaway for European nobles during the Grand Tour era. Only back then, instead of snapping selfies, they were capturing the city through poetic verses and oil paintings.

Floating in Controversy: Modern Venice grapples with its fame—shouldering the weight of tourists like Atlas with the world on his back. It's teetering between preservation and commercialization, a delicate dance on water.

Eco-Warrior Turn: As the city sinks, Venice is morphing into an unexpected role model for ecological resilience. Innovative projects like MOSE aim to protect the city from rising sea levels, showcasing a blend of history and futuristic thinking.

Don't Miss the Boat: Venice's Must-Visit Wonders

St. Mark's Basilica & Square:

Why: St. Mark's Basilica is not just an architectural masterpiece with its dazzling mosaics; it's the beating heart of Venice. The square is not only a historical marvel but also a Vaporetto hub, making it super accessible.

Tips: Go early to dodge crowds, and don't forget to climb the Campanile.

Doge's Palace:

Why: Imagine walking into a Gothic dreamland where every room makes your jaw drop a little lower. That's Doge's Palace for you. The rich history here is palpable, from the grand halls to the haunting prisons.

Tips: Try the "Secret Itineraries" tour to see the darker side of Venetian history.

Rialto Bridge & Market:

Why: You can't say you've been to Venice without visiting the Rialto Bridge. It's like saying you went to Paris but skipped the Eiffel

Tower. As for the market, imagine an open-air smorgasbord that'll have your inner foodie doing a happy dance.

Tips: Morning visits to the market are best; bridge views are stunning at sunset.

Canal Grande:

Why: Think of the Grand Canal as Venice's main artery, pumping life through its narrow lanes and into its picturesque neighborhoods. It's not just water; it's the liquid soul of the city.

Tips: Skip the gondolas and opt for a Vaporetto for a budget-friendly canal experience.

Santa Maria della Salute:

Why: A baroque masterpiece with a story of plague survival. Built as a "Thank You" note to the Virgin Mary for sparing Venice from the plague, Santa Maria della Salute is as much about history as it is about architecture.

Tips: Free entry, but toss a coin for good luck.

Galleria dell'Accademia:

Why: If you're into art and tired of hearing only about the Uffizi in Florence, this is your spot. The gallery is a sanctuary of Venetian art that often gets overshadowed by other Italian giants.

Tips: Look out for works by Titian and Canaletto.

Scuola Grande di San Rocco:

Why: If you've heard of Tintoretto, you know he's a big deal. This place is essentially his canvas, and it rivals the Sistine Chapel for sheer jaw-dropping splendor. It's the Venetian equivalent of walking into an art masterpiece.

Tips: Rent the mirror provided to save your neck from craning.

The Jewish Ghetto:

Why: The world's first ghetto; a significant piece of Venice's mosaic. The term "ghetto" originated here, and it's a poignant reminder of the community's resilience and culture.

Tips: Visit the synagogues and museums; try the Venetian-Jewish pastries.

There's Venice, and then there's Venice through the looking glass—the one with secret alleys, whispered legends, and layers of history that reveal themselves only to the truly engaged traveler. So, will you take the red Vaporetto or the blue one?

Local Etiquette

The Do's

- Greet in Italian: A simple "Buongiorno" or "Buonasera" goes a long way.
- Queue Politely: Whether it's for a Vaporetto or a scoop of gelato, patience is golden.
- Dress Respectfully: Churches require covering shoulders and knees.
- Buy Vaporetto Tickets: Seriously, they check.
- Use Both Sides of the Sidewalk: Keep to the right, especially on bridges.
- Recycle: Venetians are environmentally conscious; use separate bins for waste.

- Ask Before Photographing: Especially in stores or workshops.
- Tip Sparingly: Service is often included, but you can round up the bill.

The Don'ts

- Don't Litter: Especially not in the canals. That's a big no-no.
- Avoid Feeding Pigeons: It's actually illegal in St. Mark's Square.
- Don't Use 'Taxi' to Mean 'Vaporetto': Taxis are boats, too, but they're the expensive kind.
- Skip the Gondola Serenade: It's mostly for tourists and can be awkwardly loud.
- Don't Haggle: This isn't a bazaar.
- Avoid Eating in St. Mark's Square: Overpriced and frowned upon by locals.
- Don't Sit Randomly: Public spaces are not always for public sitting.
- No Selfie Sticks in Museums: Self-explanatory, but people still forget.

Remember, blending in is more than just camouflage; it's about resonating with the local rhythm. A faux pas here isn't just embarrassing; it can be a damper on your Venetian opera. So, toe the line but don't forget to enjoy the unique song of the city.

Key Takeaways

- Unique Vibes: Venice is a labyrinth of culture, history, and waterways, unlike any other city.
- Architectural Marvel: Built on stilts, the city grapples with a unique engineering challenge of sinking.
- Vaporetto Know-How: Mastering public water transport can enhance your experience significantly.

- Historical Lens: Venice's trade history and influence on the Renaissance add layers to its modern-day tourism.
- Must-See Spots: There are iconic places you can't afford to skip, from St. Mark's Square to the Rialto Bridge.
- Local Etiquette: Respecting local customs can make your stay enjoyable and respectful to the community.

Action Steps

- Plan Your Route: Map out the must-see spots ahead of time. Knowing where you're going saves precious vacation time.

- Vaporetto Pass: Buy a multi-day vaporetto pass online to save money and hassle. Don't forget to validate it before each journey.

- Stilt Selfie: Visit one of the lesser-known canals and take a selfie where you can see the stilts the city is built on. Post it with #VeniceUnmasked to flaunt your deep dive.

- Museum Pass: Invest in a Venice Museum Pass if you're a history buff. You'll get more bang for your buck and skip some lines.

- Eat Like a Local: Try a cicchetti bar for authentic Venetian tapas. Ask the bartender for their favorite; you won't be disappointed.

- Local Etiquette: Learn a few phrases in Italian, avoid over-touristy spots, and remember—no selfie sticks in the museums!

- Quick History Recap: Read a short article or watch a video about Venice's historical significance before you visit museums or landmarks. You'll appreciate what you're seeing so much more.

Chapter 2: A Culinary Voyage Through Venice

"Venice, the most touristy place in the world, is still just completely magic to me."

– Frances Mayes

You know how a dish can transport you to a different time and place, captivating all your senses? Now, what if I told you that we're diving into a world where even the air you breathe is infused with the aroma of fresh seafood and warm, yeasty bread? But we're not stopping at your run-of-the-mill Italian pizzeria. Oh no. We're about to embark on a gastronomic gondola ride through the hidden culinary canals of Venice. Excited? So am I. Let's eat!

Where to Find the Best Bacari (Wine Bars)

Cantina Do Mori

➤ Location: Sestiere San Polo, 429
➤ How to Get There: A short walk from the Rialto Bridge. It's tucked away in a narrow alley, so keep an eye out for the hanging copper pots outside.
➤ Local Tip: This place is famous for its "cicchetti," or small bites. Try to go early in the evening before it gets packed.

All'Arco

➤ Location: Calle Arco, San Polo 436

- ➢ How to Get There: Also near the Rialto Market. You can't miss it—just look for a crowd of locals outside.
- ➢ Local Tip: They serve some of the best "polpette" (meatballs) in town. Lunchtime is prime time here, so be prepared for a crowd.

Osteria Al Squero

- ➢ Location: Dorsoduro 943-944
- ➢ How to Get There: Take Vaporetto Line 1 to the Zattere stop.
- ➢ Local Tip: Great for people-watching as it's right across from a gondola repair yard. Ideal for an afternoon spritz.

La Cantina

- ➢ Location: Campo San Felice, Cannaregio 3689
- ➢ How to Get There: It's a 10-minute walk from the Strada Nova, along Fondamenta de la Misericordia.
- ➢ Local Tip: Known for its extensive wine selection and raw fish plates. Best to make a reservation if you're planning to go for dinner.

Vino Vero

- ➢ Location: Fondamenta Misericordia, Cannaregio 2497
- ➢ How to Get There: A bit further along the same street as La Cantina.
- ➢ Local Tip: This is a spot for the adventurous—they offer an ever-changing menu of natural wines.

Don't just walk in and grab a table—stand and mingle like a local. Many of these bacari get crowded, especially during "aperitivo" time (6–8 pm), so plan your visit accordingly. Cheers!

Local Coffee Etiquettes and Where to Find Authentic Italian Espresso

The Unwritten Rules of Coffee Drinking in Venice

No Seating, No Problem: If you sit down, you pay more. So do as the locals do: Enjoy your espresso standing at the bar.

Speed is Your Friend: Coffee drinking in Italy is like a sprint, not a marathon. Quick sips, friendly nods, and you're out!

Time Matters: Cappuccino is a morning thing. Ordering it after 11 am might earn you an eye roll from the barista.

The Real Deal Espresso Joints

Caffè del Doge

Location: Rialto, Calle dei Cinque 609

How to Get There: Right off the Rialto Bridge, close to the market.

Insider Tip: They have their own blend, and it's not for the faint-hearted. Get ready for a caffeinated punch!

Torrefazione Cannaregio

Location: Cannaregio 1337

How to Get There: Easy walk from Guglie Bridge.

Insider Tip: This is where you'll find locals sneaking in a midday espresso. They roast their own beans, so the aroma will guide you there.

Caffè Florian

Location: Piazza San Marco, 57

How to Get There: It's in St. Mark's Square; you can't miss it.

Insider Tip: This café has been around since 1720, making it Italy's oldest café. Enjoy the historical ambiance but be prepared for touristy prices.

Pasticceria Rizzardini

Location: Campo San Polo, 2775

How to Get There: About a 10-minute walk from San Toma Vaporetto stop.

Insider Tip: Get a "caffe corretto"—an espresso "corrected" with a splash of grappa. It's like Venice in a cup.

Caffè Rosso (or Il Caffè)

Location: Campo Santa Margherita

How to Get There: In the student-filled square of Santa Margherita.

Insider Tip: They offer soy milk, a rarity in traditional Italian cafés. Ideal for the lactose-challenged among us.

So, the next time you're in Venice and someone asks you if you've really experienced the city, you can say, "Espresso? Been there, sipped that."

Venetian Fish Markets: Navigating the Seas of Flavor

Why You Can't Miss It

The Venetian fish markets aren't just tables of flapping fish; they're a spectacle, a drama in several acts. There's something hypnotic about a Venetian haggling over the price of squid ink like it's a

Picasso painting. Get your elbows ready, you're diving into a cultural aquarium.

Top Picks

Rialto Fish Market

- ➢ Location: San Polo, 319
- ➢ How to Get There: Right next to the Grand Canal, a short walk from Rialto Bridge.
- ➢ Insider Tip: Go early for the freshest catch and the chance to see fishermen in knee-high boots doing what they do best.

Chioggia Fish Market

- ➢ Location: Chioggia, a town south of Venice
- ➢ How to Get There: Take a Vaporetto or a 1-hour drive from Venice.
- ➢ Insider Tip: This is where the locals go to escape tourists. Less glitzy, more fishy.

Tronchetto Market

- ➢ Location: Isola Nova del Tronchetto
- ➢ How to Get There: Vaporetto line 2, Tronchetto Mercato stop.
- ➢ Insider Tip: This is more of a wholesale market, so if you're staying a while, stock up here.

What to Buy

- ➢ Sarde in Saor: Fresh sardines to prepare this classic Venetian dish.

- ➤ Moeche: Soft-shell crabs that are a seasonal delicacy.
- ➤ Cuttlefish Ink: If you dare, this is the secret ingredient in authentic squid ink pasta.

What to Do

- ➤ Get Chatty: Talk to the fishermen. They often offer the best cooking tips.
- ➤ Look, Then Buy: Always compare the offerings at different stalls.
- ➤ Bag It: Bring your own reusable bags. Venice is aiming to be eco-friendly, and you should too.

Tips for Visiting the Rialto Market and Other Local Fish Markets

- ➤ When to Go: Aim for early morning, ideally between 7:30 and 9 a.m. The fish are fresher than a morning breeze, and you beat the tourist rush.

- ➤ Footwear: Slippery when wet! Closed-toed shoes with a good grip will keep you upright amid the aquatic chaos.

- ➤ Map It Out: Before going, have a general sense of the layout. Rialto is more than fish; there are produce and spice stalls too.

- ➤ Know Your Fish: Learn the names of the fish you're interested in, both in Italian and English. For instance, branzino is a sea bass.

- ➤ Haggle: It's not just allowed, it's expected. But remember, these folks wake up at the crack of dawn to bring you the sea's finest, so be respectful.

- ➢ Eat Before You Go: Rialto and other markets are surrounded by touristy eateries. Eat before you go or bring a snack to avoid the mediocre and overpriced temptations.

- ➢ Branch Out: Don't limit yourself to Rialto. Markets like Chioggia and Tronchetto offer a more local atmosphere.

- ➢ Bring Cash: Most stalls don't take cards. Keep some coins and small bills handy for quick transactions.

- ➢ Seasonal Delights: Ask what's in season. You might stumble upon a rare local specialty you won't find in restaurants.

- ➢ Eco-Friendly: Venice is all about sustainable tourism now. Bring a reusable bag to carry your ocean treasures.

Top Restaurant Picks for a Venetian Culinary Adventure

Osteria alle Testiere

- ➢ Location: Castello, 5801
- ➢ Local Tip: Known for seafood; make reservations well in advance.
- ➢ Getting There: A 10-minute walk from St. Mark's Square.

Da Fiore

- ➢ Location: San Polo, 2202
- ➢ Local Tip: Go for the tasting menu; it's like Venetian tapas but way chicer.
- ➢ Getting There: 15-minute vaporetto ride from San Zaccaria stop.

Antiche Carampane

- ➤ Location: San Polo, 1911
- ➤ Local Tip: You'll want the fried soft-shell crabs; trust me on this.
- ➤ Getting There: A 10-minute stroll from Rialto Bridge.

Trattoria Alla Madonna

- ➤ Location: Calle della Madonna, San Polo, 594
- ➤ Local Tip: This place is all about the Venetian classics. Don't miss the risotto.
- ➤ Getting There: A stone's throw from Rialto Market.

Corte Sconta

- ➤ Location: Castello, 3886
- ➤ Local Tip: The patio is perfect for a romantic dinner.
- ➤ Getting There: A 15-minute walk from the Arsenale vaporetto stop.

Osteria Anice Stellato

- ➤ Location: Fondamenta della Sensa, Cannaregio 3272
- ➤ Local Tip: Try their Venetian tapas called 'cicchetti.'
- ➤ Getting There: Short walk from Ca' d'Oro vaporetto stop.

Al Covo

- ➤ Location: Castello, 3968
- ➤ Local Tip: The wine pairing is exquisite; don't skip it.
- ➤ Getting There: 20-minute walk from San Zaccaria.

La Zucca

- ➤ Location: Santa Croce, 1762

- Local Tip: This spot caters to vegetarians too. The pumpkin flan is a must.
- Getting There: Easily reachable from San Stae vaporetto stop.

Eateries for Authentic Venetian Meals

Osteria La Zucca

- Location: Santa Croce, 1762
- Local Tip: Known for its vegetable dishes, a rare find in Venice.
- Getting There: San Stae vaporetto stop, then a 5-minute walk.

Osteria Al Bacco

- Location: Cannaregio, 3054
- Local Tip: Order the 'fritto misto,' a mixed fry of fish and seafood.
- Getting There: 10-minute walk from Guglie vaporetto stop.

Birraria La Corte

- Location: Campo San Polo, 2168
- Local Tip: Their pizza is some of the best in Venice. Yes, you read that right.
- Getting There: Easily accessible from the San Silvestro vaporetto stop.

Rosticceria Gislon

- Location: Calle de la Bissa, 5424
- Local Tip: Come for the 'mozzarella in carrozza,' stay for everything else.

> Getting There: 5-minute walk from Rialto vaporetto stop.

Al Timon

> Location: Fondamenta dei Ormesini, Cannaregio, 2754
> Local Tip: The riverside seating is prime real estate; get there early.
> Getting There: 10-minute walk from Guglie vaporetto stop.

Cantina Do Mori

> Location: San Polo, 429
> Local Tip: This is the oldest 'bacaro' in Venice, so you'll want the 'cicchetti' here.
> Getting There: Short walk from Rialto Market.

Vini da Gigio

> Location: Cannaregio, 3628A
> Local Tip: The 'grilled radicchio with balsamic' will change your life.
> Getting There: About a 12-minute walk from Ca' d'Oro vaporetto stop.

Osteria Enoteca Ai Artisti

> Location: Fondamenta della Toletta, Dorsoduro, 1169A
> Local Tip: Try their version of 'bigoli in salsa,' a classic Venetian dish.
> Getting There: 15-minute walk from Accademia vaporetto stop.

Key Takeaways

- Bacari Bliss: Venice's wine bars, or bacari, are essential to the local drinking culture. Don't miss them.

- Espresso Etiquette: The coffee culture in Venice is unique. Sipping espresso at the bar is the way to go.
- Fish Market Frenzy: Venetian fish markets like Rialto offer a colorful array of fresh catches and a slice of daily Venetian life.
- Local Eats: If you want to dine like a Venetian, steer clear of the tourist traps and opt for restaurants that serve authentic local meals.

Action Steps

- **Reserve a Spot:** Book a table at one of the recommended bacari during aperitivo time (6-8 pm) to ensure you get to experience the real deal.
- **Speak the Lingo:** Learn a couple of basic Italian phrases for ordering coffee. "Un caffè, per favore" is a good start!
- **Early Bird Gets the Fish:** Head to the Rialto Market early in the morning to witness the freshest catches and to avoid the tourist rush.
- **Snap a Foodie Pic:** Take photos of your authentic Venetian meals. Not just for the 'gram, but as a delicious memory to look back on.
- **Map It Out:** Save the locations of our top restaurant picks on your phone's map app. It'll come in handy when you're wandering around and hunger strikes.

So, you've just had a culinary whirlwind tour of Venice that goes beyond touristy pizza slices and overpriced gelato, haven't you? Trust me, your taste buds will thank you for the rest of your life! You've sipped authentic espresso like a local, navigated through the freshest fish markets, and had your taste of real Venetian cuisine. In short, you're no longer a tourist in this aspect—you're a bona fide Venetian foodie.

But don't pack your bags just yet! Venice has hidden corners and lesser-known spots that will make your Instagram followers green with envy. Curious? You should be!

Next Stop: "Hidden Gems of Venice." Don't miss it; we're diving deep into the secrets that this floating city holds. Stay tuned!

Chapter 3: Hidden Gems of Venice

"If you read a lot, nothing is as great as you've imagined. Venice is
— Venice is better."

– Fran Lebowitz

Hold onto your gondola hats, folks! Think Venice has no more secrets left? Ha! We've barely scratched the water's surface. Get ready to venture into a Venice you've never even imagined. Onward!

Venice's Lesser-Known Islands

Sick of the jam-packed canals of central Venice? Feel like you're on a theme park ride with no exits? Time to set sail to Venice's lesser-known islands—Murano, Burano, and Torcello.

Murano:

- Why Go: The glass-blowing capital of the world.
- Local Tip: Skip the overpriced tourist shops and head straight to the furnaces to watch masters at work.
- Getting There: Lines 4.1, 4.2, 12, 13, and N from Fondamenta Nova. Takes just about 9 minutes.

Burano:

- Why Go: Technicolor dreamland where every building looks like a scoop of gelato.
- Local Tip: This is the place to buy lace. And yes, your grandma will adore you for it.
- Getting There: Take the Vaporetto Line 12 from Fondamenta Nova ferry terminal. About 40 minutes to Burano.

Torcello:

- Why Go: The hushed atmosphere and ancient cathedrals offer a break from Venice's constant bustle.
- Local Tip: Don't miss the Devil's Bridge. No, you won't meet Satan, but the lore is intriguing.
- Getting There: Continue from Burano with Vaporetto Line 9. It's the last stop.

Libreria Acqua Alta:

- Why Go: Ever wanted to read a book in a bathtub without worrying about soggy pages? Here, you can. Books are stacked in boats, bathtubs, and waterproof bins. It's a quirky sanctuary for book lovers, where cats roam free and gondolas double as bookshelves.

- Local Tip: Look for the staircase made of books at the back; it's an Instagram hit. Also, say hi to the cats for me.

- Getting There: If you find yourself at Campo Santa Maria Formosa, just follow Calle Lunga Santa Maria Formosa right to the bookstore's entrance at Castello 5176/B. Or, if you're soaking up the atmosphere in St. Mark's Square, make your way to Piazzetta dei Leoncini and take a 5-minute stroll via Calle Canonica. Trust me, you don't want to miss this place.

A Guide to Public and Lesser-Known Private Gardens

Alright, listen up, garden enthusiasts and peace-seekers! If you thought Venice was all about canals and gondolas, you've got another thing coming. The city also offers some downright magical secret gardens—hidden havens that most tourists wouldn't even know exist. Let's lift the veil, shall we?

Giardini della Biennale

How to Get There: Take the Vaporetto Line 1 to the Giardini stop.

Tips:

- Visit during the Venice Biennale; some pavilions have their own private gardens open to the public.
- It's relatively less crowded early in the morning or late afternoon.

Orto Botanico

How to Get There: Located in the Venetian Lagoon, on San Servolo Island. Vaporetto Line 20 can get you there.

Tips:

- They offer educational tours, so call ahead and book for a deeper dive into plant life.
- Visit during spring when rare species are in bloom.

Garden of Palazzo Soranzo Cappello

How to Get There: Nestled in the Santa Croce district, it's a walkable distance from San Stae Vaporetto stop.

Tips:

- Access is by appointment only; call ahead to schedule your visit.
- Ideal for a romantic escape; this place oozes Venetian charm.

The Gardens of the Venetian Hotels

How to Get There: Various locations, but generally, a short walk from major Vaporetto stops.

Tips:

- Some hotels allow non-guests to wander in their gardens for a small fee or even free if you're having a meal there.
- Hotel Danieli and Gritti Palace have stunning gardens, FYI.

Garden of Palazzo Venart

How to Get There: A stone's throw away from the Vaporetto stop San Stae.

Tips:

- It's an excellent spot for garden-themed cocktails (yeah, you heard that right!).
- Booking a table at the on-site restaurant could grant you free access to the garden.

For the Adventurous:

Always keep an eye out for "Eden" signs around the city, these are indicators of public gardens.

Strike up a conversation with a local. You'd be surprised how many secret gardens are hidden in plain sight but known only to residents.

There you have it, a foliage-filled side of Venice you probably didn't know existed. Ready to venture into the lesser-known but incredibly enchanting parts of Venice? Keep reading, because up next, we're unmasking even more Venetian secrets!

Nightlife in Venice

Hey, night owls! If you're itching to discover the Venetian nightlife that doesn't involve selfie sticks and overpriced cocktails, you're in for a treat. Let's go on a nocturnal adventure to bars and spots where locals hang and the Aperol Spritz flows like water.

Al Timon

Location: Fondamenta dei Ormesini, Cannaregio

How to Get There: Closest Vaporetto stop is S. Marcuola.

Local Tips:

- Perfect for wine lovers; their selection is to die for.
- Try to grab an outdoor table by the canal. It's divine at sunset.

Paradiso Perduto

Location: Cannaregio, Fondamenta della Misericordia

How to Get There: A 10-minute walk from the S. Marcuola Vaporetto stop.

Local Tips:

- They often have live music, ranging from jazz to traditional Italian.
- Get there early; it fills up fast on weekends.

Il Mercante

Location: San Polo, 2564, Fondamenta Frari

How to Get There: Take the Vaporetto to San Tomà stop.

Local Tips:

- Perfect spot for cocktail aficionados. Their mixologists are top-notch.
- Ask for the cocktail of the day; it's always something unique.

Osteria Al Squero

Location: Dorsoduro, 943-944

How to Get There: The closest Vaporetto stop is Zattere.

Local Tips:

- It's a local cicchetti (tapas) bar. Order the local wines, they're affordable and exquisite.
- Ideal for a late afternoon that bleeds into an early evening; it's a daytime kind of place.

Skyline Rooftop Bar

Location: Giudecca, 810

How to Get There: Take the Vaporetto to Redentore.

Local Tips:

- A bit on the fancy side but worth it for the panoramic views.
- Dress smart-casual; this isn't your average pub.

Ai Rusteghi

Location: San Marco, 5515

How to Get There: A short walk from the Sant'Angelo Vaporetto stop.

Local Tips:

- Amazing for wine and cicchetti.
- Hidden gem alert: Tucked away in a courtyard, it's as local as it gets.

Bonus Tip: Skip the Piazza San Marco for drinks; it's a tourist trap. Instead, head towards the neighborhoods of Cannaregio and Dorsoduro for a more authentic experience.

Alright, folks, you're now armed with insider info to take on the Venetian night like a local! Ready for more? Buckle up, because next up we're delving into Venice's art scene that goes beyond just museums and galleries. You won't want to miss this!

Art and Culture Off the Beaten Path

If you're keen on soaking up Venice's art and culture without the selfie-stick wielding crowds, you're in for a treat. Let's delve into the lesser-known museums and galleries where Venetians actually go.

Ca' Pesaro

- Location: Santa Croce 2076, 30135 Venezia VE, Italy
- Tips: Skip the lines by going on weekday afternoons. Check their website for temporary exhibitions; they often feature modern art.

- How to Get There: Take the Vaporetto to the San Stae stop. The museum is a short walk away.

Punta della Dogana

- Location: Dorsoduro, 2, 30123 Venezia VE, Italy
- Tips: Enjoy the museum but save time for the view outside; it's spectacular.
- How to Get There: Vaporetto to Salute Station. It's then just a 5-minute walk.

Museo di Palazzo Grimani

- Location: Castello 4858 (Ramo Grimani), 30122 Venezia VE, Italy
- Tips: This place is an Instagram haven; lighting is excellent for period-appropriate selfies.
- How to Get There: Walking distance from Rialto Bridge or take Vaporetto to Sant'Angelo stop.

Galleria dell'Accademia

- Location: Campo della Carità, Dorsoduro 1050, 30123 Venezia VE, Italy
- Tips: Skip mornings; the light is better for viewing art in the afternoon.
- How to Get There: Vaporetto to Accademia Station.

Scuola Grande di San Rocco

- Location: San Polo, 3052, 30125 Venezia VE, Italy
- Tips: Visit during Vespers for live choral performances.
- How to Get There: A leisurely 10-minute walk from the Rialto Bridge.

Casa Goldoni

- Location: San Polo, 2794, 30125 Venezia VE, Italy
- Tips: A heaven for theater lovers; often overlooked but filled with historical costumes.
- How to Get There: Take Vaporetto to Rialto and stroll for 10 minutes.

The Jewish Museum

- Location: Campo di Ghetto Nuovo, 2902/b, 30121 Venezia VE, Italy
- Tips: The guided tours here are highly informative. A must if you're interested in Venice's Jewish history.
- How to Get There: Take Vaporetto to Guglie stop; the museum is just around the corner.

Centro Culturale Don Orione Artigianelli

- Location: Dorsoduro, 909/A, 30123 Venezia VE, Italy
- Tips: They host various workshops and cultural activities; check their schedule online.
- How to Get There: Vaporetto to Zattere.

Fortuny Museum

- Location: San Marco, 3958, 30124 Venezia VE, Italy
- Tips: This is textile and photography heaven; the exhibitions rotate frequently.
- How to Get There: Ten-minute walk from St. Mark's Square.

Key Takeaways

- Off-the-Beaten-Path Art: Places like Ca' Pesaro and Punta della Dogana offer a refreshing break from the mainstream, offering modern art and spectacular views.

- Hidden Historical Gems: Museo di Palazzo Grimani and Casa Goldoni are ideal for those looking for a deep dive into Venetian history and theater, without the crowds.

- Local Tips Matter: The right time to visit and little-known features like live choral performances at Scuola Grande di San Rocco can greatly enhance your experience.

- Ease of Access: Most of these lesser-known venues are within walking distance or a quick Vaporetto ride from popular landmarks.

- Diverse Cultural Experiences: From the Jewish Museum's enlightening guided tours to the workshops at Centro Culturale Don Orione Artigianelli, Venice offers more than just Renaissance art.

Action Steps

- Get a Venice Card: It covers your Vaporetto rides and offers free or discounted entry to various museums and cultural spots.

- Follow Local Blogs: Keep an eye on local Venice blogs for up-to-date tips on art exhibits or special events in these lesser-known museums and galleries.

- Check Availability: If you're interested in workshops or guided tours, email or call in advance to secure your spot.

- Interactive Map: Create a Google Map with pins for each of these locations. It helps you visualize your day and optimize your route.

- Ask Locals: Don't hesitate to strike up a conversation with locals. You might find out about an impromptu art show or a hidden historical gem.

There you have it—a local's guide to Venice's best-kept secrets. From the serenity of private gardens to the artistic splendors hidden away from the crowds, this city has layers just waiting for you to peel back. But what about the nuts and bolts of navigating Venice?

Stay tuned, because Chapter 4 is all about the practical stuff. We're talking tips on transportation, weather pitfalls, local scams to avoid, and a whole lot more. The fun isn't over; it's just getting more practical!

Chapter 4: Practicalities and Pitfalls

"When I went to Venice, I discovered that my dream had become- incredibly, but quite simply- my address."

– Marcel Proust

Strap yourselves in, ladies and gentlemen! Cause we're about to enter the real realm of travel planning. It's no Venice canal cruise this time; instead, we'll be navigating the choppy waters of vital know-how. Think of this as your very own Swiss Army knife filled with bundles of brilliant wisdom that will save you from any sticky situation. So, who's ready to get their hands dirty? Let's go!

When to Visit

Spring (March to May)

Pros

- Blooming flowers and mild weather.
- Fewer tourists mean a more peaceful Venice.
- Outdoor dining is back in business.

Cons

- Rainy days are frequent; bring a trendy umbrella.

Summer (June to August)

Pros

- Sunny and warm; perfect for Gondola rides.
- Festa del Redentore in July: fireworks galore!

Cons

- Crowded. Like, sardine-can crowded.
- Sweltering heat, especially in August.

Autumn (September to November)

Pros

- Mild temps and fewer crowds.
- The Venice Film Festival in September if you're into star-gazing.

Cons

- A high chance of acqua alta (high water) events.

Winter (December to February)

Pros

- Winter mist makes for incredible photos.
- Christmas in Venice is a cozy dream.

Cons

- It's chilly, so pack wisely.
- Shorter daylight hours limit your sightseeing.

Choose wisely, adventurers! Your seasonal pick can make or break your Venetian journey.

Transportation Tips

The Vaporetto

Tips

- Grab a Venezia Unica card for multiple trips. Cheaper and less hassle.
- Line 1 offers scenic views along the Grand Canal. Like a tour, but cheaper!
- Night owls, take note: Line N runs after midnight.
- Avoid buying tickets from people approaching you; they might be counterfeit. Always buy from official ticket counters or machines.

Traghetto

Tips

- It's basically a budget gondola that takes you across the canal for 2 euros.
- Stand like a local. Sitting is for tourists. Just don't fall in.
- Some operators might claim a "tourist rate." Nope, it's 2 euros for everyone. Stand your ground.

On Foot

Tips

- Maps are your bestie but get a paper one. GPS can go haywire in the narrow lanes.
- Look for "Per San Marco" signs to navigate. If lost, just follow the crowd; they're probably lost too.

Water Taxis

Tips

- Expensive but fast. Useful if you're in a rush or want a James Bond moment.
- Agree on the fare before hopping in to avoid surprises.
- Drivers might take the "scenic route" to inflate the fare. Confirm the rate and route beforehand.

Biking

Tips

- Not practical in Venice proper. Save your cycling urges for the Lido island.

Fake Tickets

- Watch out for scam artists selling "unlimited travel passes" that are nothing but worthless pieces of paper.
- Some services might slap on "baggage fees" or "night-time charges" without prior warning. Always ask for an all-inclusive price upfront.

There you go, you're now equipped to dart around Venice like a pro—or at least without getting swindled or stranded. Isn't this fun?

Accommodation: Your Home Away from Home in Venice

Budget: Hostels and Guest Houses

Casa per Ferie la Pietà: Affordable, clean, and central. Close to the Vaporetto stop.

Generator Venice: Located on Giudecca Island. It's a hostel with a bar and a youthful vibe.

Things to Know:

- Most hostels have tourist taxes not included in the online price.
- Check-in times can be strict.

Mid-Range: Boutique Hotels

Novecento Boutique Hotel: Classic Venetian style meets modern amenities. Close to major attractions.

Hotel Moresco: A little more pricey but offers free breakfast and is close to Piazzale Roma.

Things to Know:

- Mid-range hotels often have a "city tax" added to your bill.
- Booking directly might get you a room upgrade.

Luxury: Top-Tier Choices

Gritti Palace: Absolute decadence. Overlooks the Grand Canal.

Hotel Danieli: Historic charm and unmatched luxury.

Things to Know:

- Many have dress codes for dining areas.
- Concierge services can get you exclusive access to events and restaurants.

Apartments and Rentals

Airbnb: Great for longer stays and getting a local feel. But beware of scams and always read reviews.

VRBO: Similar to Airbnb but often features higher-end properties.

Things to Know:

- Check the cancellation policy.
- Make sure to ask about Wi-Fi, as not all rentals will offer it.

General Tips

- Wi-Fi: Double-check that it's free and has good speed.
- Breakfast: If not included, it could be an expensive add-on.
- Location: Staying near a Vaporetto stop will make your life easier.
- Hidden Costs: Look out for resort fees, service charges, and cleaning fees.

Common Scams and How to Avoid Them

Friendship Bracelet Scam

- What Happens: Someone ties a "friendship bracelet" around your wrist, claiming it's a gift. Then they demand payment for it. Remember, if it's good to be true, it probably is.
- How to Avoid: Keep your hands in your pockets when approached by strangers offering "gifts."

Fake Petition Scam

- What Happens: Someone asks you to sign a petition, then demands a "donation."

- How to Avoid: Politely decline or walk away without engaging.

Restaurant Scams

- What Happens: You're presented with an "English menu" with inflated prices.
- How to Avoid: Ask for the local menu, and always check the prices before ordering.

Taxi Overcharges

- What Happens: The water taxi takes a longer route, racking up a higher fare.
- How to Avoid: Agree on a price or ask for the meter to be turned on before setting off.

Pigeon Feed Scam

- What Happens: Someone puts bird feed in your hand to attract pigeons, then demands money for the feed.
- How to Avoid: Decline any "free" offerings of bird feed or similar items.

Counterfeit Souvenirs

- What Happens: Cheap, fake souvenirs peddled as authentic Venetian goods.
- How to Avoid: Stick to reputable shops for your keepsakes.

The Photo Op Scam

- What Happens: Someone offers to take your photo and then demands money or runs off with your camera.

- How to Avoid: Only hand your camera to someone you trust.

Staying alert and being aware of these common scams will save you not only money but also unnecessary headaches.

Key Takeaways

- Seasonal Insights: Each season offers unique experiences but comes with its own set of challenges. Summer is crowded but vibrant; winter is less crowded but chillier.

- Transportation: The Vaporetto system is convenient but can be confusing. Get a tourist pass for unlimited rides and always validate your ticket to avoid fines.

- Accommodation: Choices vary based on budget and travel style. Always double-check online reviews and consider the location in relation to the attractions you want to visit.

- Common Scams: From friendship bracelets to taxi overcharges, scams can ruin your day. Stay alert and know the common traps to watch out for.

Action Steps

- Check Seasonal Weather Forecasts: Before booking, consider what you want to do in Venice and how the weather might affect it.

- Plan Your Route: Familiarize yourself with the Vaporetto map and major stops before you arrive.

- Book Accommodations Early: Popular places fill up quickly, especially during high season. Book at least 3 months in advance for the best options.

- Read Reviews: Before finalizing accommodations or transportation methods, read recent reviews to avoid any unpleasant surprises.

- Stay Scam-Savvy: Keep a note in your phone of common scams so you can reference it quickly and stay alert.

- Practice Saying 'No': Whether it's to an insistent street seller or a suspiciously friendly stranger, get comfortable with saying 'no, thank you.'

Conclusion

As we close this Venetian chapter, it's clear that Venice is not just any travel destination. It's an exceptional amalgam of history, art, and culinary traditions, all floating on water. Here, beauty drips from every stucco façade, is mirrored in every canal, and is embedded in the smiles of the locals. Venice is where the past meets the present, the East shakes hands with the West, and every visitor—yes, even you—becomes part of its eternal story.

Why Venice is Exceptional

The City of Canals is unlike any other place on Earth. It's a marvel of human ingenuity, built upon wooden stilts and kept afloat by both its natural environment and the dogged determination of its people. Through its meandering canals and narrow passageways, Venice offers a tantalizing glimpse into a bygone era while remaining resolutely modern. As you've discovered in this book, Venice presents its unique face in its architecture, its markets, and even its hidden gardens and lesser-known islands like Murano and Burano.

Final Tips for Making the Most of Your Trip

- Timing is Everything: Even Venice's most touristy spots can feel intimate if you time your visits right. Early mornings and late evenings are your allies.

- Travel Light: Venice's alleys and bridges weren't designed for luggage with wheels. Pack light, or you'll curse every cobblestone.

- Speak a Little Italian: Even a simple "Buongiorno" can go a long way. Venetians appreciate it when you make the effort to speak their language, however limited your vocabulary might be.

- Respect the City: Don't litter. Venice already struggles with waste disposal, and the locals will appreciate your respect for their home.

- Book in Advance: Whether it's the Secret Itineraries tour at the Doge's Palace or a table at a top bacari, reservations are your ticket to a smoother experience.

- Budget for Extras: From entrance fees to the obligatory spritz, it's the extras that add up. Keep some spare euros for those unplanned, yet unforgettable, moments.

By now, you have the insider's roadmap to Venice, teeming with secret spots and local wisdom. You're equipped to enjoy Venice like a native, sidestepping the common pitfalls that snag most tourists. Don't let this book gather dust on your shelf. Take it with you as you hop on that Vaporetto, wander through the Rialto Market, or get lost in the maze-like streets (you will get lost, and that's okay).

So, what are you waiting for? Venice is a city of perpetual change, its beauty constantly renewed by the tides that have shaped its history. Go now, and find your own Venice, waiting amidst its waterways and winding paths.

Until then, as the Venetians say, "A presto!"—See you soon!

But before you hop on that plane, let me tease you with what's coming next—our indispensable Italian Phrase Book. From ordering a pizza like a native to mastering the fine art of Italian conversation, we'll cover it all. Trust me, you won't want to say "Arrivederci" to this upcoming guide. The Italian adventure continues, and you're just a phrase away from unlocking it all!

Bonus

Italian Phrase Book

Explore to Win

Introduction

"The name of Italy has magic in its very syllables."

— *Mary Shelley*

Ever Tried Ordering 'Spaghetti Bolognese' in Bologna and Got Eye Rolls?

You've traveled halfway across the world, camera in hand, eager to explore the fabled Italian towns, experience the iconic cuisine, and lose yourself in Renaissance art. You get to a café in Rome, and you try to order an espresso. "Uh, caffè please?" you stammer. The barista gives you a puzzled look, and suddenly you feel like you've been thrown into a Fellini movie, minus the subtitles.

And there it is—the dreaded language barrier, the invisible wall that turns would-be magical moments into cringe-worthy scenes. We've all been there, trying to mime our way through ordering food, asking directions, or heaven forbid, explaining an allergy to a skeptical-looking waiter.

What if I told you that there's a way to not just survive in Italy but actually thrive? Picture yourself negotiating prices at an open-air market in Florence with ease, making small talk with locals in a Venetian bar, or understanding why you should NEVER order a cappuccino after 11 a.m. (I know, shocking!).

This Italian Phrase Book isn't just a collection of robotic sentences—it's your secret to unlocking the soul of Italy. You'll learn phrases that are punctuated with the cadence of Italian culture, laced with local humor, and steeped in centuries-old traditions. You're not just parroting; you're participating in the culture, painting your travels with richer, more vivid hues.

Allow me to introduce myself—I've spent years teaching languages, exploring the complexities of cross-cultural communication, and committing my own fair share of embarrassing linguistic faux pas. I've distilled everything I've learned into this book, packaging it in a way that's engaging, easy to understand, and, most importantly, actionable. You're not just getting vocabulary; you're gaining a travel companion experienced in dodging the pitfalls and traps of a new language.

Your All-In-One Tool Kit

This Phrase Book provides practical dialogues for real-world situations, from haggling at markets to complaining about the hotel Wi-Fi (you can't post those Instagram pics with a snail-paced connection, right?). Plus, we've added context so you understand not just what to say but when and why to say it.

Imagine being able to:

- Connect with locals over topics that interest them (and you!).
- Navigate complicated menus without ending up with a dish you didn't expect.
- Handle emergencies with phrases that could be life-saving.
- Be confident, be understood, and be the traveler you always wanted to be.

So, are you ready to shatter that language barrier? Are you ready to go from being a lost tourist to a savvy traveler? Are you ready to Experience Italy, not just visit it?

Take the plunge. Unlock Italy with every phrase you learn and every page you turn. Don't just be another tourist snapping photos of the Colosseum. Be the traveler who knows what they're actually looking at and can talk about it in Italian.

Chapter 1: Italian 101 - The Absolute Basics

"You may have the world if I may have Italy."

— *Giuseppe Verdi*

Ready to roll up your sleeves and dive into the building blocks of the Italian language? This chapter is your jump-off point for everything essential—think of it as your Italian 101 survival kit. We'll cover the alphabet and pronunciation nuances that could save you from awkward missteps. You'll learn the absolute must-know phrases for day-to-day survival, along with a sprinkle of essential grammar—just enough to make sense without making you snooze. From greetings and polite phrases to the days of the week, we've got you covered. Let's set you up for real conversations, not just menu deciphering!

Alphabet and Pronunciation

Alright, so the Italian alphabet is pretty similar to the English one, but it's actually a bit shorter with only 21 letters. Yup, you read that right—no j, k, w, x, or y unless you're borrowing words from other languages like 'jeans' or 'yoga.'

Here's the Italian alphabet for you:

A, B, C, D, E, F, G, H, I, L, M, N, O, P, Q, R, S, T, U, V, Z.

Pronunciation Tips:

- A, E, I, O, U are the vowels, and their sounds are generally constant: A as in 'car,' E as in 'let,' I as in 'see,' O as in 'go,' and U as in 'food.'

- C is pronounced like a 'k' when it's before an 'a,' 'o,' or 'u' (think 'car'). But it's soft like 'ch' in 'cheese' when before 'e' or 'i.'

- G is hard like 'go' before 'a,' 'o,' or 'u' and soft like 'gel' before 'e' or 'i.'

- H is a silent letter; it's just there for show, like a decorative pillow.

- R is rolled. Think of it as a mini drumroll in your mouth.

- Z can be a little tricky; it's pronounced like 'ts' in 'bits' or 'ds' in 'beds,' depending on the word.

Italian Vowels, Consonants, and Common Pitfalls

Vowels:

In Italian, vowels are the straightforward guys. They have one sound and they stick to it. No dilly-dallying with different sounds like English vowels. Here's a refresher:

- A sounds like 'ah' as in 'father.'
- E is pronounced like 'eh' as in 'bet.'
- I is like 'ee' in 'see.'
- is like 'oh' in 'go.'
- U is like 'oo' in 'food.'

Consonants:

Most consonants are what you'd expect, but there are a few curveballs.

- Double Consonants: Italians love to double up their consonants. It's like emphasizing the letter. 'Palla' (ball) is not the same as 'pala' (shovel). The double 'l' means you linger on the sound a little longer.

- Gli: This is a fun one. It's a sound that doesn't exist in English. The closest approximation is the 'll' in 'million,' but not quite. It takes some practice.

- Gn: Like 'gn' in 'lasagna.' Yes, that's an Italian word too, and yes, it's pronounced 'lasa-nya.'

Common Pitfalls:

- Ignoring Double Consonants: As I mentioned, 'pala' and 'palla' are two different things. Don't shorten those double consonants; they're important.

- Adding Extra Sounds: English speakers often add an extra 'uh' sound to words ending in a vowel, like turning 'pasta' into 'past-uh.' Nope, it's just 'pasta.'

- The Tricky 'R': If you're not used to rolling your Rs, you might end up with something that sounds like the English 'd.' Practice makes perfect, so don't be shy—roll away!

- Silent 'H': Just because it's there doesn't mean you say it. 'Ho,' meaning 'I have,' is pronounced just like 'o.'

Basic Phrases for Survival

Greetings:

- Hello - Ciao (Chow)

- Good morning - Buongiorno (Bwon-jor-no)
- Good evening - Buonasera (Bwon-ah-seh-rah)
- Goodbye - Arrivederci (Ah-ree-veh-dehr-chee)

Polite Phrases:

- Please - Per favore (Pehr fah-vo-reh)
- Thank you - Grazie (Graht-zee-eh)
- You're welcome - Prego (Preh-go)
- Excuse me - Scusa (Skooh-sah)

Numbers:

- One - Uno (Oo-no)
- Two - Due (Doo-eh)
- Three - Tre (Treh)
- Four - Quattro (Kwah-tro)
- Five - Cinque (Cheen-kweh)
- Six - Sei (Seh-ee)
- Seven - Sette (Seh-teh)
- Eight - Otto (Oh-toh)
- Nine - Nove (Noh-veh)
- Ten - Dieci (Dee-eh-chee)

Days of the Week:

- Monday - Lunedì (Loo-neh-dee)
- Tuesday - Martedì (Mar-teh-dee)
- Wednesday - Mercoledì (Mehr-co-leh-dee)
- Thursday - Giovedì (Joh-veh-dee)
- Friday - Venerdì (Veh-nehr-dee)
- Saturday - Sabato (Sah-bah-toh)
- Sunday - Domenica (Doh-meh-nee-kah)

Months:

- January - Gennaio (Jehn-nyah-yo)
- February - Febbraio (Fehb-brah-yo)
- March - Marzo (Mar-tso)
- April - Aprile (Ah-pree-leh)
- May - Maggio (Mah-joh)
- June - Giugno (Joo-nyoh)
- July - Luglio (Loo-lyoh)
- August - Agosto (Ah-goh-sto)
- September - Settembre (Seht-tehm-breh)
- October - Ottobre (Oht-toh-breh)
- November - Novembre (Noh-vehm-breh)
- December - Dicembre (Dee-chehm-breh)

Basic Questions:

- What's your name? - Come ti chiami? (Koh-meh tee kee-ah-mee?)
- How are you? - Come stai? (Koh-meh stai?)
- Where is the bathroom? - Dov'è il bagno? (Doh-veh eel bahn-yoh?)
- How much does it cost? - Quanto costa? (Kwan-toh koh-stah?)

Personal Pronouns:

- I - Io (Ee-oh)
- You (singular) - Tu (Too)
- He/She/It - Lui/Lei (Loo-ee / Lay)
- We - Noi (Noy)
- You (plural) - Voi (Voy)
- They - Loro (Loh-roh)

Personal pronouns are the bread and butter of most sentences. Here's a tip: Italians often drop the subject pronoun because the verb form usually makes it clear who the subject is. So instead of saying "Io vado" for "I go," you might just hear "Vado."

Articles:

- The (masculine singular) - Il (Eel)
- The (feminine singular) - La (Lah)
- The (masculine plural) - I (Ee)
- The (feminine plural) - Le (Leh)
- A or An (masculine) - Un (Oon)
- A or An (feminine) - Una (Oo-nah)

The Italian language uses gendered articles, which isn't common in English. So, it's essential to know whether a noun is masculine or feminine. Generally, nouns ending in -o are masculine, and those in -a are feminine, but there are exceptions.

Quick Tips:

- Gender Agreement: Make sure adjectives agree in gender and number with the noun they describe.
  - Example: "Il caffè caldo" (the hot coffee) vs. "La pizza calda" (the hot pizza).
- Article Drop: Unlike English, Italian sometimes drops the article for general statements.
  - Example: "Amo caffè" (I love coffee), no "the" necessary!

Quick Tips for Mastering Gender and Plurals

- Nouns Ending in 'o' or 'a': These usually follow the gender rules. Words ending in '-o' are often masculine, while those ending in '-a' are usually feminine. To make them plural, change the '-o' to '-i' and the '-a' to '-e.'

- o Example: Ragazzo (boy) becomes Ragazzi (boys), and Ragazza (girl) becomes Ragazze (girls).

- **Nouns Ending in 'e':** These can be either masculine or feminine, but the plural for both is '-i.'
  - o Example: Amore (love, masculine) becomes Amori (loves), and Notte (night, feminine) becomes Notti (nights).

- **Don't Assume Gender:** Some words are exceptions. Like 'problema' is masculine even though it ends in 'a.'

- **The Articles:** 'Il' is for singular masculine nouns, 'la' for singular feminine nouns, and 'lo' for singular masculine nouns that start with 's,' followed by another consonant, or with 'z,' 'pn,' 'ps.'
  - o Example: Il ragazzo (the boy), La ragazza (the girl), Lo studente (the student).

- **Plural Articles:** 'I' is the plural of 'il' and 'lo,' and 'le' is the plural of 'la.'
  - o Example: I ragazzi (the boys), Le ragazze (the girls).

Exercises

Multiple Choice

1. Which of the following vowels is always pronounced the same in Italian?
   a) A
   b) E
   c) I
   d) U

2. How do you say "hello" in Italian?
   a) Saluto
   b) Salve
   c) Bonjour
   d) Hallo

3. What is the Italian word for "one"?
   a) Due
   b) Tre
   c) Uno
   d) Quattro

4. Which personal pronoun refers to "you" (informal singular)?
   a) Lei
   b) Lui
   c) Io
   d) Tu

5. How do you say "thank you" in Italian?
   a) Prego
   b) Ciao
   c) Grazie
   d) Scusa

Fill in the Blanks

1. _____ is the formal word for "you" in Italian.
2. To say "Good evening," you would say _____.
3. The Italian word for "please" is _____.
4. "Arrivederci" means _____ in English.
5. The plural form of 'la donna' is 'le _____.'

True or False

1. "Buongiorno" can mean both "good morning" and "good afternoon."
2. "Come stai?" is a formal way to ask, "How are you?"
3. "Per favore" translates to "Thank you."
4. "Io" means "I" in Italian.
5. In Italian, all nouns have a gender.

Answer Key

Multiple Choice:

1. a) A
2. b) Salve
3. c) Uno
4. d) Tu
5. c) Grazie

Fill in the Blanks:

1. Lei
2. Buona sera
3. Per favore
4. Goodbye

5. Donne

True or False:

1. True
2. False. It's informal.
3. False. It means "Please."
4. True
5. True

Key Takeaways

- Alphabet and Pronunciation: Italian uses the Latin alphabet with a few variations in pronunciation. It's phonetic, meaning you pronounce words how they're spelled.
- Vowels and Consonants: Italian vowels are pure and constant, but beware of double consonants—they can change the word's meaning.
- Survival Phrases: Memorize basic greetings, polite phrases, numbers, and days of the week to navigate daily life.
- Pronouns and Articles: Master the basic pronouns like 'io' and 'tu,' and the common articles 'il,' 'la,' and 'lo' to build simple sentences.
- Gender and Plurals: Pay attention to the word endings. Typically, '-o' and '-i' are masculine, '-a' and '-e' are feminine. But there are exceptions, so stay alert.

Action Steps

- Practice Pronunciation: Use online resources or language apps to hear and practice Italian sounds daily.
- Flashcards for Phrases: Create digital or paper flashcards for the survival phrases. Review them during idle moments— while in line or waiting for coffee.

- Interactive Learning: Use language learning apps to reinforce the pronouns, articles, and basic phrases you've learned.
- Sentence Building: Try building simple sentences using the pronouns and articles covered. You can use a translation app to check your work.
- Gender and Plurals: Make a cheat sheet for word endings that signify gender and plurals. Refer to it until these become second nature to you.
- Community Engagement: Join online forums or local meetups to practice your Italian. Even a little practice with native speakers can go a long way.
- Daily Application: Try using Italian words and phrases in your daily life—greet your pet, count your steps, or even name the foods in your fridge in Italian.

You've just taken a significant first step in cracking the Italian language code. From pronunciation to essential phrases, this chapter has laid the groundwork for your linguistic journey in Italy. Imagine not having to point and mime your way through a restaurant menu; we've got you covered!

Up next? A feast for the senses as we dive into the delicious world of Italian food and dining. Get ready to eat your way through Italy, one word at a time. Stay tuned!

Chapter 2: Food and Dining - Buon Appetito!

"Life is a combination of magic and pasta"

— *Federico Fellini*

Get ready to tantalize your taste buds as we delve into the culinary scene of Italy—a country where food is not just sustenance but an art form. In this chapter, we'll guide you through decoding menus so you'll never accidentally order a cow stomach again (unless you want to). Learn the secrets of ordering like a local, navigate the nuances of Italian table manners, and even get the lowdown on tipping etiquette. Consider this your passport to dining in Italy. No translation apps required. Buon appetito!

Decoding Menus: The Lay of the Land

- Antipasti (Starters): Italians kick off their meals with antipasti, which could range from olives to cured meats. Memorize "antipasti" and you won't accidentally skip to the main course.

- Primi (First Courses): Usually pasta, risotto, or soup. Know that "al dente" means the pasta is cooked so that it still has a bite to it. Don't expect mushy pasta; that's not the Italian way.

- Secondi (Main Courses): Meat or fish dishes, often served without sides ("contorni"), which you order separately.

- Dolci (Desserts): Tiramisu, anyone?

- Bevande (Beverages): Wines are usually listed as "vini rossi" (red wines) or "vini bianchi" (white wines).

Language Focus & Hacks

- Dietary Restrictions: If you're vegetarian, the word to remember is "vegetariano." Gluten-free is "senza glutine."

- Understand Local Ingredients: Acquaint yourself with key Italian ingredients like "aglio" (garlic), "cipolla" (onion), "manzo" (beef), "pollo" (chicken), and so on.

- Common Pitfall: "Peperoni" in Italian refers to bell peppers, not the spicy sausage you might be thinking of. If you want that, ask for "salsiccia piccante."

- Learn Cooking Methods: Terms like "alla griglia" (grilled), "al forno" (baked), and "fritto" (fried) can be your best friends.

- 'Senza' is Your Friend: This word means 'without.' If you want a dish but need to remove an ingredient, just say the ingredient's name followed by "senza." For instance, "senza aglio" means without garlic.

- Ask for Recommendations: "Cosa consiglia?" means "What do you recommend?" It's always a good idea to ask for local favorites.

Common Dishes

Pasta Dishes

- Spaghetti Carbonara: Creamy pasta with pancetta, eggs, and Pecorino Romano cheese.

- Penne Arrabbiata: Penne pasta in a spicy tomato sauce with garlic and red chili peppers.
- Tagliatelle al Tartufo: Pasta with truffle sauce.
- Fettuccine Alfredo: Fettuccine pasta in a sauce made from butter and Parmesan.

Meat Dishes

- Osso Buco: Braised veal shanks cooked with vegetables, white wine, and broth.
- Saltimbocca: Veal, prosciutto, and sage, rolled up and cooked in dry white wine and butter.
- Pollo alla Cacciatora: Chicken stewed with tomatoes, onions, and herbs.

Seafood Dishes

- Fritto Misto: A mixed-fried seafood platter.
- Cioppino: Seafood stew with various types of fish, shellfish, and a tomato-based broth.

Vegetarian Options

- Melanzane alla Parmigiana: Eggplant Parmesan.
- Gnocchi Sorrentina: Potato dumplings in tomato sauce, mozzarella, and basil.
- Risotto ai Funghi: Mushroom risotto.

Desserts

- Tiramisu: Layered dessert made from coffee-soaked ladyfingers and a mascarpone cheese mixture.

- Cannoli: Tube-shaped shells of fried pastry dough filled with sweetened ricotta.
- Panna Cotta: A creamy dessert flavored with vanilla and served with a fruit compote.

Drinks

- Espresso: A strong coffee shot.
- Negroni: A cocktail made with gin, vermouth, and Campari.
- Aperol Spritz: A cocktail of prosecco, Aperol, and soda water.

Ordering Like a Local

Know the Meal Structure

Italians take their food seriously, and meals usually have a structure. They often start with an "antipasto" (starter), move to a "primo" (first course, usually pasta or risotto), then a "secondo" (second course, usually meat or fish), and sometimes even a "contorno" (side dish). Dessert, or "dolce," usually follows. So, if you want to blend in, consider ordering a full-course meal.

How to Ask

When you're ready to order, a simple "Vorrei..." ("I would like...") followed by the dish's name will do. If you want to sound even more local, just say the name of the dish you want and add "per favore" (please) at the end.

Ordering Coffee

Remember, ordering a cappuccino after 11 AM is a tourist move. Italians only drink milky coffee in the morning. After meals, it's usually an espresso, known simply as "caffè."

Understand Portion Sizes

In Italy, food is about quality over quantity. Don't expect gigantic portions. If you're dining with someone, consider sharing dishes to taste more flavors.

Special Requests

Italians are proud of their dishes, so asking for substitutions might not go down well. However, if you have dietary restrictions, say it upfront. The term for gluten-free is "senza glutine," and for vegetarians, it's "vegetariano."

Local Specialties

Always ask for the specialty of the house, "la specialità della casa." This is usually a dish the restaurant takes particular pride in and is often a local dish you won't find elsewhere.

Closing the Meal

After you're done, ask for "Il conto, per favore" to get the bill. Don't rush this part; enjoy some "digestivo" like limoncello or grappa to close the meal.

Food Ordering Vocabulary & Phrases

- Menu, per favore ("meh-noo, pehr fah-vo-reh") - Menu, please
- Vorrei ordinare ("vor-ray or-dee-nar-eh") - I'd like to order
- Antipasto ("ahn-tee-pahs-toh") - Starter
- Primo ("pree-moh") - First course
- Secondo ("seh-kon-doh") - Second course
- Contorno ("kohn-tohr-noh") - Side dish
- Dolce ("dohl-cheh") - Dessert
- Acqua ("ahk-wah") - Water

- Vino rosso/bianco ("vee-noh roh-soh/bee-ahn-koh") - Red/white wine
- Birra ("beer-rah") - Beer
- Senza ghiaccio ("sen-zah gyah-cho") - Without ice
- Posso avere il conto? ("poh-soh ah-veh-reh eel kohn-toh") - Can I have the bill?
- Porto via ("pohr-toh vee-ah") - Take away
- Sono allergico/a a... ("soh-noh ahl-lehr-gee-koh/ah") - I am allergic to...
- Senza glutine ("sen-zah gloo-tee-neh") - Gluten-free
- Vegetariano/a ("veh-je-tah-ree-ah-no/ah") - Vegetarian (M/F)
- È piccante? ("eh peek-kahn-teh") - Is it spicy?
- Una tavola per due, per favore ("oo-nah tah-voh-lah pehr doo-eh, pehr fah-vo-reh") - A table for two, please
- Posso vedere la lista dei vini? ("poh-soh veh-deh-reh lah lees-tah day vee-nee") - Can I see the wine list?
- Suggerimenti? ("soo-gehr-ree-men-tee") - Any suggestions?
- Mi porti...? ("mee pohr-tee") - Could you bring me...?
- Più pane, per favore ("pyoo pah-neh, pehr fah-vo-reh") - More bread, please
- Il caffè ("eel kah-feh") - Coffee
- Un cappuccino ("oon kah-poo-chee-noh") - A cappuccino
- Un espresso ("oon ehs-prehs-soh") - An espresso
- Una porzione di... ("oo-nah pohr-tsee-oh-neh dee") - A serving of...
- Ho fame ("oh fah-meh") - I'm hungry
- Sono sazio/a ("soh-noh sah-tsee-oh/ah") - I'm full (M/F)
- È delizioso/a! ("eh deh-lee-tsyoh-soh/ah") - It's delicious! (M/F)
- Non mi piace ("nohn mee pyah-cheh") - I don't like it
- È incluso il servizio? ("eh een-kloo-zoh eel sehr-vee-tsyoh") - Is service included?

- Dividiamo il conto ("dee-vee-dee-ah-moh eel kohn-toh") - Let's split the bill
- Va bene così ("vah beh-neh koh-zee") - Keep the change
- Pasta al dente ("pah-stah ahl dehn-teh") - Pasta cooked "to the tooth" (firm)
- Sugo ("soo-goh") - Sauce
- Carne cruda ("kahr-neh kroo-dah") - Raw meat
- Pesce crudo ("peh-sheh kroo-doh") - Raw fish
- Formaggi misti ("fohr-mah-jee mees-tee") - Assorted cheeses
- Vorrei un bicchiere di... ("vor-ray oon beek-kee-eh-reh dee") - I'd like a glass of...
- Un tavolo all'aperto ("oon tah-voh-loh ahl-lah-pehr-toh") - An outdoor table

Exercises

Multiple Choice

1. What is "antipasto" in Italian cuisine?
   - a) Dessert
   - b) Main Course
   - c) Appetizer
   - d) Drink

2. How would you ask for the menu in Italian?
   - a) "Un caffè, per favore."
   - b) "Il conto, per favore."
   - c) "Il menu, per favore."
   - d) "Una birra, per favore."

3. What is the Italian word for water?
   - a) Vino
   - b) Succo
   - c) Acqua
   - d) Latte

4. Which phrase would you use to order food?
   - a) "Vorrei ordinare."
   - b) "Mi scusi."
   - c) "Vado via."
   - d) "Grazie mille."

5. How do you say "vegetarian" in Italian?
   - a) Vegano
   - b) Vegetariano
   - c) Carnivoro
   - d) Onnivoro

Fill in the Blanks

1. "_____" means "please" in Italian.
2. To say "cheers" or "to good health," you would say "_____."
3. The Italian word for "bread" is "_____."
4. A small Italian coffee is called a "_____."
5. "_____" is the correct way to ask for the bill.

True or False

1. Tipping is mandatory in Italian restaurants.
2. "Posso avere il conto?" is how you ask where the restroom is.
3. It's considered rude to ask for ketchup in Italy.
4. "Buon appetito" is the Italian way to say "enjoy your meal."
5. It's customary to say "grazie" even before tasting the food.

Answer Key

Multiple Choice:

1. c) Appetizer
2. c) Il menu, per favore
3. c) Acqua
4. a) Vorrei ordinare
5. b) Vegetariano

Fill in the Blanks:

1. Per favore
2. Salute
3. Pane
4. Espresso
5. Il conto, per favore

True or False:

1. False. It's appreciated but not mandatory.
2. False. It's how you ask for the bill.
3. True
4. True
5. False. Say "grazie" after you've tasted and enjoyed it.

Awesome, you're now equipped to dine like a true Italian! From decoding menus to ordering with finesse, you've got the lingo down pat. And hey, let's not forget the all-important tipping etiquette. You're not just a tourist anymore; you're a well-fed traveler savoring Italy one dish at a time.

Ready for the next leg of our journey? Trust me, you don't want to miss this. We're diving into the world of "Shopping and Services"— the right phrases can make or break a deal. Whether it's haggling for a Venetian mask or asking for directions, we've got you covered. So, let's continue our Italian adventure, shall we?

Chapter 3: Shopping and Services

"Italian culture is so deeply soaked in an appreciation of the good things in life."

— *Mariska Hargitay*

We are now pivoting from delicious Italian dishes to the alluring world of shopping and services. Let's explore how to haggle for the perfect souvenir, book a last-minute hotel room, and even navigate an Italian pharmacy—all without breaking a sweat or getting lost in translation. Your Italian journey is about to get even more rewarding.

Shopping Vocabulary

- Negozio - Shop (Ney-goh-tzyoh)
- Acquistare - To buy (Ah-kwee-stah-ray)
- Vendere - To sell (Ven-de-ray)
- Sconto - Discount (Skon-toh)
- Cassa - Cash register (Kahs-sah)
- Contanti - Cash (Kon-tahn-tee)
- Carta di Credito - Credit Card (Kahr-tah dee Kray-dee-toh)
- Prezzo - Price (Preh-tzoh)
- Scontrino - Receipt (Skon-tree-noh)
- Prova - Fitting Room (Pro-vah)
- Taglia - Size (Tahl-yah)
- Abbigliamento - Clothing (Ahb-beel-yah-men-toh)
- Alimentari - Grocery (Ah-lee-men-tah-ree)
- Farmacia - Pharmacy (Fahr-mah-chee-ah)
- Aperto - Open (Ah-pehr-toh)
- Chiuso - Closed (Kee-oo-so)

- Orario di apertura - Opening hours (Or-ah-ree-oh dee ah-pehr-too-rah)
- Offerta - Offer, Sale (Of-fehr-tah)
- Carrello - Cart (Kar-rel-loh)
- Scaffale - Shelf (Skaf-fah-leh)

Common Types of Stores

- Supermercato - Supermarket
- Enoteca - Wine shop
- Ferramenta - Hardware store
- Libreria - Bookstore
- Gioielleria - Jewelry store
- Calzoleria - Shoe store
- Pasticceria - Pastry shop
- Profumeria - Perfume shop
- Salumeria - Deli
- Ottica – Optician

Clothing Items

- Maglia - Sweater
- Camicia - Shirt
- Pantaloni - Trousers
- Vestito - Dress
- Scarpe - Shoes
- Cappello - Hat
- Cravatta - Tie
- Guanti - Gloves
- Gonna - Skirt
- Cappotto – Coat

Other Shopping Items

- Portafoglio - Wallet
- Orologio - Watch
- Borsa - Bag/Purse
- Trucco - Makeup
- Telefono - Phone
- Computer - Computer
- Libro - Book
- Souvenir - Souvenir
- Candela - Candle
- Giocattolo – Toy

At the Market

- Quanto costa? - How much does it cost? (Kwahn-toh koh-stah)
- Posso provare? - Can I try this? (Pohs-soh proh-vah-rey)
- C'è uno sconto? - Is there a discount? (Cheh oo-noh skon-toh)
- Vorrei un chilo di... - I would like a kilogram of... (Vohr-ray oon kee-loh dee)
- Mi può dare un po' di... - Can you give me some of... (Mee pwaw dah-rey oon poh dee)
- È fresco? - Is it fresh? (Eh freh-skoh)
- Accetto solo contanti - I only accept cash. (Ach-et-toh soh-loh kon-tahn-tee)
- Avete...? - Do you have...? (Ah-veh-teh)
- È troppo caro - It's too expensive. (Eh troh-poh kah-roh)
- Potrebbe fare un prezzo migliore? - Could you give a better price? (Poht-reb-beh fah-rey oon preht-zoh my-lyoh-reh)
- Prendo questo - I'll take this. (Prehn-doh kweh-stoh)
- Non mi interessa, grazie - I'm not interested, thank you. (Nohn mee in-teh-rehs-sah, graht-zee-eh)

- Dov'è il mercato? - Where is the market? (Doh-veh eel mehr-kah-toh)
- Cosa consiglia? - What do you recommend? (Koh-zah kon-seel-yah)
- Ne vorrei due - I would like two. (Neh vohr-ray doo-eh)
- Sono allergico/a a... - I'm allergic to... (Soh-noh al-lehr-jee-koh/ah ah)
- Potete impacchettare? - Can you wrap it up? (Poht-eh-teh eem-pahk-keht-tah-reh)
- Scontrino, per favore - Receipt, please. (Skon-tree-noh, pehr fah-voh-reh)
- Ho cambiato idea - I changed my mind. (Oh kahm-byah-toh ee-deh-ah)
- Quando chiudete? - When do you close? (Kwahn-doh kyoo-deh-teh)

Phrases for Haggling and Bagging the Best Deals

- È l'ultimo prezzo? - Is this the final price? (Eh lool-tee-moh preht-zoh)
- Può fare meglio? - Can you do better? (Pwoh fah-rey meh-lyoh)
- Troppo caro, grazie - Too expensive, thank you. (Troh-poh kah-roh, graht-zee-eh)
- Me lo può lasciare a...? - Can you let me have it for...? (Meh loh pwoh lahs-chah-rey ah)
- Mi può fare uno sconto? - Can you give me a discount? (Mee pwoh fah-rey oo-noh skon-toh)
- Non ho abbastanza soldi - I don't have enough money. (Nohn oh ahb-bah-stahn-tsah sohl-dee)
- È incluso nel prezzo? - Is it included in the price? (Eh een-kloo-zoh nehl preht-zoh)
- Ci posso pensare? - Can I think about it? (Chee pohs-soh pehn-sah-rey)

- Accettate carte? - Do you accept cards? (Ah-cheht-tah-teh kahr-teh)
- Vorrei comprarne due per... - I'd like to buy two for... (Vohr-ray kohm-prahr-neh doo-eh pehr)
- Questo è il mio limite - This is my limit. (Kweh-stoh eh eel my-oh lee-mee-teh)
- Posso pagare in contanti? - Can I pay in cash? (Pohs-soh pah-gah-rey een kon-tahn-tee)
- Ce l'hai in un altro colore? - Do you have it in another color? (Cheh lah-ee een oon ahl-troh koh-loh-rey)
- Ha difetti? - Does it have any flaws? (Hah dee-feht-tee)
- È autentico? - Is it authentic? (Eh ow-tehn-tee-koh)
- È in saldo? - Is it on sale? (Eh een sahl-doh)
- Se ne prendo due, mi fa sconto? - If I buy two, will you give me a discount? (Seh neh prehn-doh doo-eh, mee fah skon-toh)
- Posso provarlo? - Can I try it on? (Pohs-soh proh-vahr-loh)
- Facciamo cinquanta e cinquanta? - How about we split the difference? (Fah-chyah-moh cheen-kwahn-tah eh cheen-kwahn-tah)
- Accetto, è un affare! - I accept, it's a deal! (Ah-cheht-toh, eh oon ahf-fah-reh)

Remember, haggling is a negotiation, so keep your tone friendly but assertive. Happy shopping!

Beauty Services

- Prenotazione - Appointment (Preh-noh-tah-zee-oh-neh)
- Taglio di capelli - Haircut (Tahl-yoh dee kah-pehl-lee)
- Manicure - Manicure (Mah-nee-kyoor)
- Pedicure - Pedicure (Peh-dee-kyoor)
- Trattamento viso - Facial treatment (Trah-tah-mehn-toh vee-zoh)

- Vorrei un massaggio - I would like a massage (Vohr-ray oon mahs-sahj-yoh)
- Avete prodotti biologici? - Do you have organic products? (Ah-veh-teh proh-doh-tee byoh-loh-jee-chee)

Health Services

- Medico - Doctor (Meh-dee-koh)
- Farmacia - Pharmacy (Fahr-mah-chee-ah)
- Prescrizione - Prescription (Preh-skree-zee-oh-neh)
- Dentista - Dentist (Dehn-tees-tah)
- Sono allergico a... - I am allergic to... (Soh-noh ahl-lehr-jee-koh ah)
- Mi sento male - I feel sick (Mee sehn-toh mah-leh)
- Dove si trova l'ospedale? - Where is the hospital? (Doh-veh see troh-vah lohs-peh-dah-leh)
- Ho bisogno di un medico - I need a doctor (Oh by-sohn-yoh dee oon meh-dee-koh)
- Esame del sangue - Blood test (Eh-zah-meh dehl sahn-gweh)

Postal Services

- Ufficio postale - Post Office (Oof-fee-chio pohs-tah-leh)
- Vorrei spedire questo pacco - I would like to send this package. (Vor-ray speh-dee-ray kweh-stoh pahk-koh)
- Raccomandata - Registered mail (Rah-koh-man-dah-tah)
- Francobollo - Stamp (Fran-koh-bol-lo)
- Busta - Envelope (Boo-stah)
- Dove è la cassetta delle lettere? - Where is the mailbox? (Doh-veh eh lah kahs-seht-tah dehl-leh leht-teh-reh)

Telecommunication Services

- SIM prepagata - Prepaid SIM card (Seem preh-pah-gah-tah)

- Ricarica - Top-up (Ree-kah-ree-kah)
- Credito esaurito - Out of credit (Creh-dee-toh eh-sow-ree-toh)
- Internet illimitato - Unlimited internet (Een-tehr-neht eel-lee-mee-tah-toh)
- Abbonamento - Subscription (Ahb-boh-nah-men-toh)
- Hai WiFi? - Do you have WiFi? (Eye Wee-Fee?)
- Qual è la password del WiFi? - What's the WiFi password? (Kwahl eh lah pahs-word dehl Wee-Fee?)

Digital Etiquette: Social Media and Texting in Italian

- What's up? - Come stai? (Koh-meh sty?)
- LOL (Laugh Out Loud) - haha (same as in English, but sometimes written as "ahah")
- BRB (Be Right Back) - Torno subito (Tohr-noh soo-bee-toh)
- See you soon - A presto! (Ah preh-stoh)
- Selfie - Selfie (Same as in English)
- Tag me - Taggami (Tahg-gah-mee)
- Unfriend - Rimuovi amicizia (Ree-mwoh-vee ah-mee-chee-tsyah)
- Slide into DMs - Invia un messaggio privato (Een-vyah oon meh-sah-jee-oh pree-vah-toh)
- Is this your post? - Questo è il tuo post? (Kwes-toh eh eel two-oh pohst?)

Emoji Etiquette: Italians love using emojis to express emotions and to emphasize points. Feel free to use them, but don't overdo it; keep it relevant to the context.

Politeness: Italians value politeness even in informal settings like social media. Phrases like "per favore" (please) and "grazie" (thank you) go a long way.

Punctuation: Excessive exclamation marks or question marks can be considered impolite or overly dramatic. Use them sparingly.

Local Hashtags: Pay attention to popular Italian hashtags like #Buongiorno (Good Morning) or #Cena (Dinner) to engage with local trends.

DMs and Friend Requests: It's polite to send a quick hello and introduce yourself when sending a friend request or direct message to someone you don't know well.

Exercises

Multiple Choice

1. What is "negozio" in English?
   a) Bank
   b) Hotel
   c) Store
   d) Restaurant

2. How do you ask for the price of an item?
   a) "Quanto costa?"
   b) "Dov'è?"
   c) "Posso provare?"
   d) "È aperto?"

3. What is "sconto" in English?
   a) Exit
   b) Sale
   c) Gift
   d) Size

4. Which phrase means "Do you accept credit cards?"
   a) "Accettate carte di credito?"
   b) "È incluso il servizio?"
   c) "Avete una taglia più grande?"
   d) "Posso avere un sacchetto?"

5. What does "farmacia" mean?
   a) Bakery
   b) Pharmacy
   c) Bookstore
   d) Shoe store

Fill in the Blanks

1. "_____" is the Italian word for "open."
2. When asking if a store has more sizes, you say "Avete altre _____?"
3. "_____" is how you'd say "market" in Italian.
4. "_____" means "thank you" in Italian.
5. To ask for a bag, you would say "Posso avere un _____?"

True or False

1. "Carta di credito" means cash.
2. It's common to haggle prices in Italian markets.
3. "Chiuso" means the store is open.
4. You can say "Mi scusi" to get someone's attention in a store.
5. "Contrattare" is the Italian word for haggling.

Answer Key

Multiple Choice

1. c) Store
2. a) Quanto costa?
3. b) Sale
4. a) Accettate carte di credito?
5. b) Pharmacy

Fill in the Blanks

1. Aperto
2. Taglie
3. Mercato
4. Grazie
5. Sacchetto

True or False

1. False. It means credit card.
2. True
3. False. It means the store is closed.
4. True
5. True

You're now equipped to navigate the hustle and bustle of Italian shopping scenes and take care of all your postal and telecommunication needs. But what happens when you find yourself in social situations? Ah, that's where the fun begins! From dinner parties to local festivals, the next chapter will teach you how to blend in and master the art of Italian socializing. Ready to unlock your inner Italian socialite? Keep reading!

Chapter 4: Navigating Social Situations

"Italy is a dream that keeps returning for the rest of your life."

— *Anna Akhmatova*

We are diving into the social dance of Italy—Navigating Social Situations. Ever been caught in an awkward moment, unsure of the local social cues? Or maybe you've committed a cultural faux pas and didn't even realize it? Fear not! We're covering essential social vocabulary, decoding body language, and giving you the inside scoop on Italian social norms. From first encounters to fond farewells, you'll learn how to gracefully handle social interactions like a true Italian. Stay with us, because you won't want to miss the deep-dive into Italian social graces coming up next!

Starting Conversations

- What's your name? - Come ti chiami? (Koh-meh tee kee-ah-mee?)
- How old are you? - Quanti anni hai? (Kwahn-tee ahn-nee eye?)
- What do you do for a living? - Di cosa ti occupi? (Dee koh-sah tee oh-koo-pee?)
- Where are you from? - Di dove sei? (Dee doh-veh say?)
- Do you come here often? - Vieni qui spesso? (Vyeh-nee kwee spehs-soh?)
- Have we met before? - Ci siamo già incontrati? (Chee see-ah-moh jah een-kohn-trah-tee?)

- What's new? - Cosa c'è di nuovo? (Koh-sah cheh dee noo-vo?)
- How's it going? - Come va? (Koh-meh vah?)
- How has your day been? - Com'è stata la tua giornata? (Kohm-eh stah-tah lah too-ah jor-nah-tah?)
- Do you mind if I join you? - Ti dispiace se mi unisco a te? (Tee dees-pee-ah-cheh seh mee oo-nee-sho ah teh?)

Introducing Yourself

- Hi, my name is [Your Name] - Ciao, mi chiamo [Tuo Nome] (Chow, mee kee-ah-mo [Tuo Nome])
- I'm from [Your Country] - Sono di [Tuo Paese] (Soh-no dee [Tuo Paese])
- I'm a [Your Profession] - Sono un/una [Tua Professione] (Soh-no oon/oo-nah [Tua Professione])
- I'm here for [Reason] - Sono qui per [Ragione] (Soh-no kwee pehr [Ragione])

Asking Basic Questions

- What's your name? - Come ti chiami? (Koh-meh tee kee-ah-mee?)
- Where are you from? - Di dove sei? (Dee doh-veh say?)
- How old are you? - Quanti anni hai? (Kwahn-tee ahn-nee eye?)
- What do you do? - Cosa fai? (Koh-sah figh?)
- Do you like [Activity/Food/etc.]? - Ti piace [Attività/Cibo/etc.]? (Tee pee-ah-che [Attività/Cibo/etc.]?)

Public Transportation Phrases

- Bus Stop - Fermata dell'autobus (Fehr-mah-tah dehl-l'ow-toh-boos)

- Train Station - Stazione ferroviaria (Stah-tsyoh-neh fehr-roh-vee-ah-ree-ah)
- Ticket - Biglietto (Beel-yet-toh)
- One-way ticket - Biglietto di sola andata (Beel-yet-toh dee soh-lah ahn-dah-tah)
- Round-trip ticket - Biglietto andata e ritorno (Beel-yet-toh ahn-dah-tah eh ree-tohr-noh)
- Subway - Metropolitana (Meh-troh-poh-lee-tah-nah)

Asking for Directions

- How do I get to [place]? - Come arrivo a [posto]? (Koh-meh ahr-ree-voh ah [poh-stoh]?)
- Is it far? - È lontano? (Eh lohn-tah-noh?)
- Go straight - Vai dritto (Vigh dreet-toh)
- Turn left/right - Gira a sinistra/destra (Jeer-ah ah seen-eest-rah/deh-st-rah)
- At the corner - All'angolo (Ahl-l'ahn-goh-loh)
- Excuse me, can you help me? - Scusami, puoi aiutarmi? (Scoo-sah-mee, pwoh-ee ahyoo-tahr-mee?)

Key Phrases For Not Getting Lost

- I'm lost. - Sono perso/a. (Soh-noh pehr-soh/ah)
- Can you show me on the map? - Puoi mostrarmi sulla mappa? (Pwoh-ee moh-strahr-mee sool-lah mahp-pah)
- Where is the nearest [place]? - Dove è il più vicino [posto]? (Doh-veh eh eel pyoo vee-chee-noh [poh-stoh]?)
- I need to go to [place]. - Devo andare a [posto]. (Deh-voh ahn-dah-reh ah [poh-stoh])
- Is it within walking distance? - È raggiungibile a piedi? (Eh rah-june-jee-bee-leh ah pyeh-dee?)
- Please write it down for me. - Per favore, me lo scrivi? (Pehr fah-vo-reh, meh loh skree-vee)

- I'm trying to find [address]. - Sto cercando di trovare [indirizzo]. (Stoh chehr-cahn-doh dee troh-vah-reh [een-dee-reez-zoh])
- Can you guide me? - Puoi guidarmi? (Pwoh-ee gwee-dahr-mee)
- Is this the right way to [place]? - È questa la strada giusta per [posto]? (Eh kweh-stah lah strah-dah joo-stah pehr [poh-stoh]?)

At the Hotel

- Do you have a room available? - Avete una camera disponibile? (Ah-veh-teh oo-nah kah-meh-rah dees-poh-nee-bee-leh)
- I have a reservation. - Ho una prenotazione. (Oh oo-nah preh-noh-tah-zee-oh-neh)
- What time is check-in/check-out? - A che ora è il check-in/check-out? (Ah keh oh-rah eh eel chehk-een/chehk-owt)
- I'd like a room with a view. - Vorrei una camera con vista. (Vohr-ray oo-nah kah-meh-rah kohn vees-tah)
- Can I have the Wi-Fi password? - Posso avere la password del Wi-Fi? (Pohs-soh ah-veh-reh lah pahs-word dehl Wee-Fee)
- Where is the elevator? - Dove si trova l'ascensore? (Doh-veh see troh-vah lahs-chehn-soh-reh)
- I need an extra pillow. - Ho bisogno di un cuscino extra. (Oh bee-sohn-yo dee oon koos-chee-noh ehks-trah)
- How much does it cost per night? - Quanto costa a notte? (Kwahn-toh koh-stah ah noht-teh)
- Is breakfast included? - La colazione è inclusa? (Lah koh-lah-tsee-oh-neh eh een-kloo-sah)
- I need to extend my stay. - Devo prolungare il mio soggiorno. (Deh-voh proh-loon-gah-reh eel mee-oh soh-jyohr-noh)

Checking In

- Is my room ready? - La mia camera è pronta? (Lah mee-ah kah-meh-rah eh prohn-tah)
- I'd like to check-in. - Vorrei fare il check-in. (Vohr-ray fah-reh eel chehk-een)
- Requesting Amenities
- Can I have some extra towels? - Posso avere degli asciugamani extra? (Pohs-so ah-veh-reh dehl-yee ah-shoo-gah-mah-nee ehks-trah)
- Could you send up room service? - Potreste mandare il servizio in camera? (Poht-reh-steh mahn-dah-reh eel sehr-vee-tsyoh een kah-meh-rah)
- Is there a gym in the hotel? - C'è una palestra in albergo? (Cheh oo-nah pah-lehs-trah een ahl-behr-goh)

Troubleshooting Issues

- The air conditioner isn't working. - L'aria condizionata non funziona. (Lah-ree-ah kohn-dee-tsyoh-nah-tah nohn foon-tsyoh-nah)
- I can't connect to the Wi-Fi. - Non riesco a connettermi al Wi-Fi. (Nohn ryeh-skoh ah kohn-neht-tehr-mee ahl Wee-Fee)
- The room is too noisy. - La camera è troppo rumorosa. (Lah kah-meh-rah eh trohp-poh roo-moh-roh-sah)

Events and Entertainment

- What time does the event start? - A che ora inizia l'evento? (Ah keh oh-rah een-tsyah leh-vehn-toh)
- Is there a dress code? - C'è un codice di abbigliamento? (Cheh oon koh-dee-cheh dee ahb-bee-glee-ah-mehn-toh)

- Are tickets still available? - Ci sono ancora biglietti disponibili? (Chee soh-noh ahn-koh-rah beel-yeh-tee dees-poh-nee-bee-lee)
- Where can I buy tickets? - Dove posso comprare i biglietti? (Doh-veh pohs-soh kohm-prah-reh ee beel-yeh-tee)
- Is it an outdoor event? - È un evento all'aperto? (Eh oon eh-vehn-toh ahl-lah-pehr-toh)
- Is there a bar? - C'è un bar? (Cheh oon bahr)
- Can I take photos? - Posso fare delle foto? (Pohs-soh fah-reh dehl-leh foh-toh)
- Who is performing tonight? - Chi si esibisce stasera? (Kee see eh-see-bee-cheh stah-seh-rah)
- What genre is the music? - Di che genere è la musica? (Dee keh zheh-neh-reh eh lah moo-see-kah)

How to Ask For Tickets, Show Timings, And Express Likes or Dislikes

- May I have two tickets, please? - Posso avere due biglietti, per favore? (Pohs-soh ah-veh-reh doo-eh beel-yeh-tee, pehr fah-voh-reh)
- How much is a ticket? - Quanto costa un biglietto? (Kwahn-toh koh-stah oon beel-yeh-toh)
- What time does the show start? - A che ora inizia lo spettacolo? (Ah keh oh-rah een-tsyah loh speht-tah-koh-loh)
- Is it a matinee or an evening show? - È uno spettacolo pomeridiano o serale? (Eh oo-noh speht-tah-koh-loh poh-meh-ree-dee-ah-noh oh seh-rah-leh)
- Is the show appropriate for children? - Lo spettacolo è adatto ai bambini? (Loh speht-tah-koh-loh eh ahd-aht-toh ahy bahm-bee-nee)
- Do you offer any discounts? - Offrite degli sconti? (Ohf-freet-eh dehl-yee skohn-tee)

- I enjoyed the show. - Mi è piaciuto lo spettacolo. (Mee eh pyah-choo-toh loh speht-tah-koh-loh)
- I didn't like it much. - Non mi è piaciuto molto. (Nohn mee eh pyah-choo-toh mohl-toh)
- Do you have shows every weekend? - Avete spettacoli ogni fine settimana? (Ah-veh-teh speht-tah-koh-lee oh-nyee feeh-neh seht-tee-mah-nah)

Exercises

Multiple Choice

1. How do you say "Goodbye" in Italian?
   a) Hola
   b) Bonjour
   c) Arrivederci
   d) Adiós

2. How would you ask for someone's name in Italian?
   a) Come ti chiami?
   b) Como estas?
   c) Comment ça va?
   d) Wie heißt du?

3. What is the Italian phrase for "How much does it cost?"
   a) Was kostet das?
   b) Combien ça coûte?
   c) Quanto costa?
   d) Cuánto cuesta?

4. How would you ask for directions to the train station?
   a) Dove si trova la farmacia?
   b) Dove si trova la stazione ferroviaria?
   c) Where is the bathroom?
   d) Où est la gare?

5. What should you say when you like a show?
   a) Lo odio
   b) Mi è piaciuto
   c) Es war schrecklich
   d) C'était terrible

Fill in the Blanks

1. If you're asking someone how they are, you might say
   "_____?"
2. When lost, you could ask, "Posso avere _____?"
3. For requesting two tickets, you say "Posso avere _____
   biglietti, per favore?"
4. The Italian phrase for "Good morning" is "_____."
5. When checking into a hotel, you'd likely say "Ho una
   _____."

True or False

1. "Arrivederci" means "See you later."
2. "Dove si trova" is the phrase for asking where something is
   located.
3. "Non mi è piaciuto" means you enjoyed something.
4. In Italian, you'd ask for directions by saying "Where is the
   train station?"
5. "Quanto costa" asks about the cost of something.

Answer Key

Multiple Choice:

1. c) Arrivederci
2. a) Come ti chiami?
3. c) Quanto costa?
4. b) Dove si trova la stazione ferroviaria?
5. b) Mi è piaciuto

Fill in the Blanks:

1. Come stai

2. indicazioni
3. due
4. Buongiorno
5. prenotazione

True or False:

1. True
2. True
3. False. It means you did not enjoy it.
4. False. The correct phrase is "Dove si trova la stazione ferroviaria?"
5. True

Conclusion

"Travel and change of place impart new vigor to the mind."

— *Seneca*

As we say in Italy, 'Dove finisce il gioco, vengono fuori i cerotti.' When the game ends, the bandages come off. Now that you've reached the end of this book, it's time to rip off the training wheels and immerse yourself in real conversations.

When we started this journey, I bet you were feeling the frustration of trying to navigate through Italian cities, trying to order pasta without accidentally asking for 'squid ink,' or simply yearning for a deeper connection with locals that goes beyond 'Ciao!' That's a pain point that almost every traveler or language enthusiast experiences, and that's what this book was designed to solve.

In Chapter 1, 'Italian 101 - The Absolute Basics,' we took baby steps. We went through the ABCs—literally. Understanding the alphabet and pronunciation sets the foundation for learning any language. We also ventured into vowels, consonants, and the often-confusing Italian pronouns and articles like 'il, la, lo.' We even took a slight detour into the world of Italian grammar, focusing on gender and plurals. Not too bad for starters, eh?

But knowing the alphabet won't feed you; knowing how to order food will. That's why Chapter 2, 'Food and Dining - Buon Appetito!' was all about gastronomical communication. Whether you're vegetarian, gluten-intolerant, or an adventurous eater, knowing how to decode Italian menus and order like a local can make or break your dining experience. We also discussed tipping, because nobody wants to be that tourist who doesn't tip or, worse, tips too much.

Once we got you fed, it was time for some retail therapy in Chapter 3, 'Shopping and Services.' Here, you learned how to navigate markets and malls, haggle like a pro, and even ask for specific beauty treatments or health services. Don't underestimate the power of being able to ask for a 'taglio di capelli' (haircut) the way you like it.

Finally, Chapter 4, 'Navigating Social Situations,' got you out and about. We went through how to strike up conversations, ask for directions, manage hotel check-ins, and even get your groove on at Italian entertainment events.

Knowing local phrases is like having a secret key to the city. It unlocks experiences, relationships, and a deeper understanding of the culture that a mere 'Ciao' or 'Grazie' can never provide. But remember, this is just the tip of the iceberg; languages evolve, and the more you practice, the better you'll get.

So, what's next? Keep learning, keep practicing, and most importantly, start planning that trip to Italy if you haven't already. Trust me, the gelato tastes better when you can ask for your favorite flavor in Italian.

As your journey with the Italian language continues, don't forget to revisit this book. It's a resource that grows in value the more you use it. Consider it your pocket translator, your Italian confidant, and your guide to not just surviving but thriving in Italy.

So go ahead, and immerse yourself in the culture, the language, the food, and the fashion that is uniquely Italian. You're now armed with the basics to not only survive but also enjoy an enriching travel experience.

Buon viaggio e a presto! (Have a good trip and see you soon!)

For more exciting and in-depth guides on mastering the Italian language and other travel tips, don't forget to check out our other publications. Your journey has only just begun, so why stop now?

Book Description

Dreaming of an unforgettable Italian adventure but overwhelmed by the thought of planning your trip? Ever wondered how you can relish the food, converse with locals, and move around Rome, Florence, or Venice like a seasoned traveler?

You're not alone. Italy is a top travel destination that can overwhelm even the most seasoned globetrotter. The art, the food, the architecture, the language—where to start? That's why We've compiled everything you need to know in one incredible book bundle. With years of travel experience under our belt and a flair for language teaching, We've got you covered!

In this book bundle, you'll discover:

- The must-visit spots in Rome, Florence, and Venice that only locals know about.
- The essential Italian phrases that will make your trip smoother.
- How to dine in Italy without offending any local customs.
- Your shopping guide to scoring authentic Italian goods.
- A sneak peek into the culture and social norms—get the real Italian experience!
-

Are you worried about language barriers? Concerned that you might miss out on the best hidden spots? Don't worry!

Even if you've never stepped foot outside of your hometown, these books are meticulously designed to guide you through Italy as if you've been there a thousand times.

So why this bundle? Because it's not just a travel guide, it's a comprehensive toolkit for experiencing Italy at its finest—like an insider, not a tourist.

Imagine yourself sipping on an authentic espresso in a Roman café, or navigating the canals of Venice like a pro, or enjoying a sumptuous Florentine meal with the confidence of a local. That's what you get when you arm yourself with the right knowledge.

So, if you're ready to unlock the secret to a stress-free and enriching Italian experience, hit the "add to cart" button *NOW* and embark on an Italian adventure you'll never forget!

Made in the USA
Middletown, DE
21 December 2023

46631680R00136